Keto Meal Prep 2018

4 Manuscripts – Keto Meal Prep, Keto Meal Prep For Beginners,A Complete Ketogenic Diet for Beginners, Ketogenic Vegetarian

by

Helen Robbins

Keto Meal Prep 2018

Table of Contents

KETO MEAL PREP

KETO MEAL PREP FOR BEGINNERS

A COMPLETE KETOGENIC DIET FOR BEGINNERS

KETOGENIC VEGETARIAN

INTRODUCTION

In the United States, the obesity epidemic continues to rise. 38% of our adult population are considered obese. Another 33% of persons are considered overweight. This is according to The Centers For Disease Control and Prevention.

The numbers are even higher for women. Women, because of our child-bearing bodies, have other factors we must contend with. Elevated estrogen levels and different female hormones have our bodies already at a higher fat percentage. Obesity is medically defined as having a body index (BMI) of more than 30%. Personally, I have dieted almost my entire adult life. I'm now over the age of 50. I began to look for a better way to approach food Ketogenic is a diet known as a very low carb diet. It is a high fat, moderate protein and low carb intake diet. It turns your body into a fat burning machine. There is a much more scientific explanation but basically you force your body to produce ketones in the liver to be used for energy. On the opposite end, eating foods high in carbs and sugars your body will produce glucose and raise insulin levels.

Although ketogenics is new to many, it was around as early as the 1920s. The keto lifestyle can have a healthful effect on serious health conditions, like cardiovascular diseases and diabetes. It improves levels of HDL cholesterol.

To enter into ketosis, you need to reduce your carbs to under 50 grams a day. Ideally 25-30 carbs max. Your fat intake should be about 75% of your meals and about 15% protein. It varies from person to person, but with consistency you should be able to get into ketosis within 3-14 days.

When you consume a high amount of carbohydrates your metabolism spends most of the time burning carbs for fuel. You never get to burn stored fat. If you decrease the amount of available carbs, your body must switch to burning your fat.

CHAPTER ONE

THE BASIC PRINCIPLES OF THE KETOGENIC DIET

The ketogenic diet is a diet based on a process called ketosis. It is a specific state of the body, which is characterized by an elevated level of ketones in the blood, which occurs due to the conversion of fats into fatty acids and ketones. This occurs when the body gets only very small amounts of carbohydrates over a certain period of time. When you start with this type of diet, your body goes through several changes. 24-48 hours after the beginning of this diet, the body starts to use ketones in order to use the energy stored in fat cells more efficiently. In other words, the primary source of energy becomes fat (fatty acids), instead of carbohydrates (glucose). Because of that, during ketosis it is not a problem to eat food with higher amounts of fat, than would otherwise seem reasonable. This way the body is rapidly losing weight (specifically fat). In addition, the loss of muscle tissue (proteins) is minimal, since the vast majority of food consumed during ketosis, also contains relatively large amounts of proteins that are good for your muscles.

Although ketosis is the basis of the ketogenic type of diet, in its strictest form it doesn't need to be kept for long. The state of ketosis can be held up until the body weight is just a few pounds higher than the one that is desired. Then foods with higher amounts of carbohydrates are gradually introduced (rice, beans). In this period, it would be very useful to keep a food intake diary in which daily amounts of taken carbs would be noted. That way you can find the maximum amount of daily carbs that still allow you not to gain weight. Once you discover this parameter, you will no longer have weight-related problems, because you will certainly learn to take account of the calories and amounts of carbs, proteins and fats that you consume daily. That way you will get to know your body better, in terms of the maximum "allowable" daily intake. Because of that, we could say that the ketogenic diet is, in a way, a procedure for learning habits that will ensure that you never return to the old potentially problematic overweight levels.

There are many types of ketogenic diets, but they all have in common one basic principle: the intake of high amounts of proteins and fats, and minimal amounts of carbohydrates. Which exact diet you will choose isn't as important, as long as it will allow you to enter ketosis, which is the basis of the biological mechanism that will help you lose weight efficiently.

Low carb diets have advantages and disadvatages.

The reason low carb has a bad rap is that people say they are low carb, but really aren't. It's like saying you're low calorie while eating a bowl of ice cream with a donut on top. The people who give low carb a bad name do not follow the basic principle of low carb: a constant, steady stream of carbs that have a total during the day of less than a set amount, usually 100g, and all of the carbs come from fruits and vegetables. Of course, some diets are more strict and I myself keep to below 70g per day.

So, who are these people who say they are low carb, but really aren't? Well, they starve themselves of carbs, focus on meats and fats only and then pig out on sugar on the weekends. Then they start all over again. These people are cranky, depressed and miserable. Plus, they aren't losing a pound. They blame the diet and not the dieter who isn't doing it right.

Doctors hate the low carb diet because of these people. You see, when you starve yourself of something, then pig out, you force your body to shift it's metabolism from ketogenic (protein) metabolism to carbohydrate metabolism quickly, and it doesn't like it. It leads to a stressed liver, heart and brain. It produces lots of cortisol, which causes us to hold onto fat and store even more. It layers plaque in our arteries to help reduce the stress. It harms the kidneys because of the toxic burden of switching back and forth.

The focus on meats and fats deprives the body of vital nutrients and the organs start to break down. This kind of dieting makes people sick. This is where many of the myths of the low carb diet come from: these people who are not doing low carb at all.

For those who want to do it right, it requires discipline. It requires long periods of constant, steady streams of carbs, without spikes or indulgences. In fact, it is one of the healthiest diets to be on. Lower carb is the basis of all healthy diets: Mediterranean, vegetarian, diabetic, Atkins and all the others.

BASIC PRINCIPLES OF THE KETOGENIC DIET

Doing it right goes like this:

Set your carbs: I recommend no less than 60g/day unless under the care of a nutritionist.

Plan your day around your fruits and vegetables: I recommend no less than 5 servings per day

Make sure those fruits and vegetables are within your carb counts.

Flavor with herbs and spices – as many as possible (they have 0 carbs!)

Fill in with local, organic or natural meats and healthy fats.

Planning this way will allow you to consume many foods, enough to keep you full and happy and provide all the nutrition you require.

There is only one problem with eating low carb the right way. Fruits and vegetables do not have convenient packages to know exactly how many carbs are in them. A pepper is usually about 6g per serving but can be as low as 4g in the spring to nearly 10g in the fall. But that's OK, you don't need to be that precise, so long as fruits and vegetables make up the biggest part of your diet.

CHAPTER TWO

WHY KETO MEALS

Keto diets have really caught on in the past year and a half and for good reason. It's a great way to not only shed those unwanted pounds quickly, but also a great way to get healthy and stay that way. For those that have tried the Keto Diet and are still on it, it's more than just a diet. It's a way of life, a completely new lifestyle. But like any major shift in our lives it is not an easy one, and it takes an incredible amount of commitment and determination.

Good for some but not for all? Although a ketogenic diet has been used to greatly improve people's quality of life, there are some out there who do not share the majority's way of thinking. But why is that exactly? Ever since we can remember we have been taught that the only way to get rid of the extra weight was to quit eating the fat-filled foods that we are so accustomed to eating every day. So instructing people to eat healthy fats (the key word is healthy), you can certainly understand why some people would be skeptical as to how and why you would eat more fat to achieve weight loss and achieve it fast. This concept goes against everything we have ever known about weight loss.

How Keto Started. Discovered by endocrinologist Rollin Woodyatt in 1921 when he found that 3 water-soluble compounds named aceture, B-hydroxybutyrate and acetoacetate (known together as ketone bodies) were produced by the liver as a result of starvation or if the person followed a diet rich with high fat and very low carbs. Later on that year a man from the Mayo Clinic by the name of Russel Wilder named it the "Ketogenic Diet" and used it to treat epilepsy in young children with great success. But because of advancements in medicine it was replaced.

What Does A Ketogenic Diet Look Like? When the average person eats a meal rich in carbs, their body takes those carbs and converts them into glucose for fuel. Glucose is the body's main source of fuel when carbs are present in the body; on a keto diet there are very low if any carbs consumed which forces the body to utilize other forms of energy to keep the body functioning properly. This is where healthy fats come into play; with the absence of carbs the liver takes fatty acids in the body and converts them into ketone bodies.

An ideal keto diet should consist of:

- 70-80% Fat

- 20-25% Protein

- 5-10% Carbs

You should not be eating more than 20g of carbs per day to maintain the typical Ketogenic diet. I personally ate less than 10g per day for a more drastic experience but I achieved my initial goals and then some. I lost 28 lbs in a little under 3 weeks.

What Is Ketosis? When the body is fueled completely by fat it enters a state called "ketosis" which is a natural state for the body. After all of the sugars and unhealthy fats have been removed from the body during the first couple of weeks, the body is now free to run on healthy fats. Ketosis has many potential benefits related to rapid weight loss, health or performance. In certain situations like type 1 diabetes excessive ketosis can become extremely dangerous, whereas in certain cases paired with intermittent fasting it can be extremely beneficial for people suffering from type 2 diabetes. Substantial work is being conducted on this topic by Dr. Jason Fung M.D. (Nephrologist) of the Intensive Dietary Management Program.

What I Can and Can't Eat. For someone new to keto it can be very challenging to stick to a low-carb diet, even though fat is the cornerstone of this diet you should not be eating any and all kinds of fat. Healthy fats are essential, but what is healthy fat you might ask. Healthy fats would consist of grass-fed meats, (lamb, beef, goat, venison), wild caught fish and seafood, pastured pork & poultrys. Eggs and salt free butters can also be ingested. Be sure to stay away from starchy vegetables, fruit, and grains. Processed foods are in no way accepted in any shape or form on the ketogenic diet. Artificial sweeteners and milk can also pose a serious issue.

Reasons to Avoid Low Carb Diets

Low carb (carbohydrate), high protein diets are the latest dieting craze. However, before you jump on the band wagon, you may want to consider a few things:

1. Low carb (ketogenic) diets deplete the healthy glycogen (the storage form of glucose) stores in your muscles and liver. When you deplete glycogen stores, you also dehydrate, often causing the scale to drop significantly in the first week or two of the diet. This is usually interpreted as fat loss when it's actually mostly from dehydration and muscle loss. By the way, this is one of the reasons that low carb diets are so

popular at the moment – there is a quick initial but deceptive drop in scale weight.

Glycogenesis (formation of glycogen) occurs in the liver and muscles when adequate quantities of carbohydrates are consumed – very little of this happens on a low carb diet.

Glycogenolysis (breakdown of glycogen) occurs when glycogen is broken down to form glucose for use as fuel.

2. Depletion of muscle glycogen causes you to fatigue easily, and makes exercise and movement uncomfortable. Research indicates that muscle fatigue increases in almost direct proportion to the rate of depletion of muscle glycogen. Bottom line is that you don't feel energetic and you exercise and move less (often without realizing it) which is not good for caloric expenditure and basal metabolic rate (metabolism).

3. Depletion of muscle glycogen leads to muscle atrophy (loss of muscle). This happens because muscle glycogen (broken down to glucose) is the fuel of choice for the muscle during movement. There is always a fuel mix, but without muscle glycogen, the muscle fibers that contract, even at rest to maintain muscle tone, contract less when glycogen is not

immediately available in the muscle. Depletion of muscle glycogen also causes you to exercise and move less than normal which leads to muscle loss and the inability to maintain adequate muscle tone.

Also, in the absence of adequate carbohydrate for fuel, the body initially uses protein (muscle) and fat. The initial phase of muscle depletion is rapid, caused by the use of easily accessed muscle protein for direct metabolism or for conversion to glucose (gluconeogenesis) for fuel. Eating excess protein does not prevent this because there is a caloric deficit.

When insulin levels are chronically too low as they may be in very low carb diets, catabolism (breakdown) of muscle protein increases, and protein synthesis stops.

4. Loss of muscle causes a decrease in your basal metabolic rate (metabolism). Metabolism happens in the muscle. Less muscle and muscle tone means a slower metabolism which means fewer calories burned 24 hours-a-day.

5. Your muscles and skin lack tone and are saggy. Saggy muscles don't look good, cause saggy skin, and cause you to lose a healthy, vibrant look (even if you've also lost fat).

6. Some proponents of low carb diets recommend avoiding carbohydrates such as bread, pasta, potatoes, carrots, etc. because of they are high on the glycemic index, causing a sharp rise in insulin. Certain carbohydrates have always been, and will always be the bad guys: candy, cookies, baked goods with added sugar, sugared drinks, processed/refined white breads, pastas, and rice, and any foods with added sugar.

These are not good for health or weight loss.

However, carbohydrates such as fruits, vegetables, legumes, whole grain breads and pastas, and brown rice are good for health and weight loss. Just like with proteins and fats, these carbohydrates should be eaten in moderation. Large volumes of any proteins, fats or carbohydrates are not conducive to weight loss and health.

The effect of high glycemic foods is often exaggerated. It does matter, but to a smaller degree than is often portrayed. Also, the total glycemic effect of foods is influenced by the quantity of that food that you eat at a sitting. Smaller meals have a lower overall glycemic effect. Also, we usually eat several types of food at the same time, thereby reducing the average glycemic index of the meal, if higher glycemic foods are eaten.

Also, glycemic index values can be misleading because they are based on a standard 50 grams of carbohydrate consumed.

It wouldn't take much candy bar to get that, but it would take four cups of carrots. Do you usually eat four cups of carrots at a meal?

Regular exercisers and active people also are less effected by higher glycemic foods because much of the carbohydrate comsumed is immediately used to replenish glycogen stores in the liver and muscle.

By the way, if you're interested in lowering insulin levels, there is a great way to do that – exercise and activity.

7. Much of the weight loss on a low carb, high protein diet, especially in the first few weeks, is actually because of dehydration and muscle loss.

8. The percentage of people that re-gain the weight they've lost with most methods of weight loss is high, but it's even higher with low carb, high protein diets. This is primarily due to three factors:

> A. You have lost muscle. With that comes a slower metabolism which means fewer calories are burned 24 hours-a-day. A loss of muscle during the process of losing

weight is almost a guarantee for re-gaining the lost weight, and more.

B. You re-gain the healthy fluid lost because of glycogen depletion.

C. It's difficult to maintain that type of diet long-term.

D. You have not made a change to a long-term healthy lifestyle.

9. Eating too much fat is just not healthy. I know you've heard of people whose blood levels of cholesterol and triglycerides have decreased while on a low carb, high protein diet. This often happens with weight loss, but it doesn't continue when you're on a diet high in fat.

There are literally reams of research over decades that clearly indicates that an increase in consumption of animal products and/or saturated fat leads to increased incidences of heart disease, strokes, gallstones, kidney stones, arthritic symptoms, certain cancers, etc. For example, in comparing countries with varying levels of meat consumption, there is a direct relationship between the volume of meat consumption in a country and the incidence of digestive cancers (stomach, intestines, rectal, etc.).

Fat is certainly necessary, and desirable in your diet, but you should eat mostly healthy fats and in moderation.

Manufactured/synthetic "low fat" foods with lots of added sugar are not the answer. Neither are manufactured/synthetic "low carb" foods with artificial sweeteners or added fat. By the way, use of artificial sweeteners has never been shown to aid in weight loss and they may pose health problems.

10. As someone recently told me, "it must work, people are losing weight". People that are truly losing fat on low carb, high protein diets, are doing so because they are eating fewer calories – that's the bottom line. There is no magic – the same can be done on a healthy diet.

11. Low carb diets are lacking in fiber. Every plant-based food has some fiber. All animal products have no fiber. A lack of fiber increases your risk for cancers of the digestive tract (because transit time is lengthened) and cardiovascular disease (because of fiber's effect on fat and cholesterol). It also puts you at a higher risk for constipation and other bowel disorders.

12. Low carb diets lack sufficient quantities of the the many nutrients/phytonutrients/antioxidants found in

fruits, vegetables, legumes, and whole grains, necessary for health and aiding in the prevention of cancer and heart disease. In fact, you need these nutrients even more so when you're consuming too much fat as is often the case on a low carb, high protein diet.

13. Amercans already consume more than twice the amount of protein needed. Add to that a high protein diet and you have far too much protein consumption. By the way, most people don't realize that all fruits, all vegetables, all whole grains, and all legumes also contain protein. Animal products contain larger quantities of protein, but that may not be a good thing.

Excess dietary protein puts you at a higher risk for many health problems: gout (painful joints from high purine foods which are usually high protein foods), kidney disease, kidney stones, osteoporosis (excess dietary protein causes leeching of calcium from the bones). By the way, countries with lower, healthier intakes of protein also have a decreased incidence of osteoporosis.

14. Low carb, high protein diets cause an unhealthy physiological state called ketosis, a type of metabolic acidosis. You may have heard the phrase, "fat burns in the flame of carbohydrate". Excess acetyl CoA

cannot enter the Krebs Cycle (you remember the old Krebs Cycle) due to insufficient OAA. In other words, for fat to burn efficiently and without production of excess toxic ketones, sufficient carbohydrate must be available. Ketosis can lead to many health problems and can be very serious at it's extreme.

15. Bad breath. Often called "keto breath" or "acetone breath", it's caused by the production of acetones in a state of ketosis. So why the low carb, high protein craze? I believe there are several reasons.

> A. Weight loss (mostly muscle and muscle fluid) is often rapid during the first few weeks. This causes people to think they're losing fat rapidly.

> B. It gives you "permission" to eat the "bad foods": bacon, eggs, burgers, steak, cheese, etc. and lots of fat.

CHAPTER THREE

HOW TO AVOID COMMMON MISTAKES FOR BEGINNERS

Considering the variety of low carb diet variations out there, it can be hard to decide which one to stick to. For the most part, the low carb approach is perfect if you require to lose 30lbs or more. The most basic low carb diet that seems to work most effectively for individuals works as follows: for nine days you limit your carbohydrate intake to 30 grams everyday. On the 10th day, during the night time, you're allowed a high carbohydrate splurge, but you don't start consuming carbs until after 4pm. After this 10 day period your carb nights are spread out roughly once per week.

It sounds uncomplicated, doesn't it? If you've done any dieting in the past you've quite possibly tinkered around with diets similar to this. However, there are several common pitfalls that either impede progress or cause some people to make hardly any progress. I'll list a couple of them and give some remedies for how to prevent yourself from falling into these traps.

It is very effortless to ingest way too many carbs mainly because of the places you purchase meals. These days a lot of people don't cook and prepare their meals. Many individuals dine out, and although you have a "low carb salad" you will probably find yourself going over your limit by having food that has too many carbs without realizing it. A number of the low fat dressings have approximately 7-10g of carbs, and from time to time when you order a salad they will put greater than three portions. A good practice that my clients use is as simple as just getting the restaurant to put the dressing on the side and all you have to do is separate out a serving.

Going overboard on dairy is yet another frequent blunder. Unless you have a history of enduring dairy well, I strongly recommend most clients to refrain from it entirely when starting off. For most people, dairy can supercharge your urge for food which will cause you to consume too much.

Overeating is the next obvious pitfall. Unless you're eating a lot of whole foods and foods that have marginal processing, it may be easy to overeat. To guarantee your results, its best that you be wary of how much you consume. This is especially true if you're having difficulty experiencing fast enough results. Many of the processed "low carb" foods are very tasty which will either cause you to overeat that food, or just heighten your desire for food for the day which may lead to overeating.

Not receiving a good mix of fat and protein can lead to headaches or the dreaded "ketogenic flu" or keto flu. The signs are a bad throbbing headache and lots of fatigue. This develops as your body adjusts to not having enough carbs using fat instead. When your fat intake is lacking your body may have challenges getting sufficient energy. Don't be afraid of fat, just ensure to keep your saturated fat in check. Sources like avocados, olive oil and coconut oil are fantastic sources. Nuts are okay, you just have to look at the amount of carbs depending on the types of nuts or seeds you take in.

You may still have your steak and various fatty cuts of animal meat. Just make certain that fat sources vary. Coconut oil is a fat that consists of MCTs which your system is able to digest quickly to be used as energy. Other fats take longer to break down and by the time you get that keto flu headache, it can be far too late before symptoms are taken care of.

30 DAYS LOW CALORIES DIET PLAN

A 30 Day Diet Plan is most suitable for people that want to lose weight in a short period. There are several good diet plans available. A detox plan is a good example. A seven day detox meal plan is probably the best choice to lose the most weight in a week. It is a good way to cleanse the body of harmful toxins and lose weight at the same time.

Obviously the main concept of this plan is to consume very little calories. For this meal plan to be successful all of the calories must be counted before being consumed, and a person needs to figure out how many calories they should consume in a day to loose the amount of weight they want. This is calculated by height, weight, gender, age, and body mass index.

This meal plan falls under the category of detox diets. Although the name suggests that any amount of any kind of food can be eaten, in actuality only certain foods are allowed on certain days. The foods allowed to be consumed are vegetables, fruits, lean meat, and skim milk. It is important to drink a lot of water (8 glasses per day).

The Cabbage Soup Diet is another example of a diet plan. It is also considered to be a detox diet.

This meal plan consists of very little fat, all of the cabbage soup a person wants to eat, fruits, vegetables, and lean meat. Cabbage is a negative energy vegetable, this means the body burns more calories eating and digesting it than the cabbage contains. Therefore the more cabbage that is eaten the more weight a person will lose.

The recipe to make the cabbage soup is very simple:

1 small cabbage,

6 medium onions,

7 tomatoes,

2 green peppers.

Chop all the vegetables into small pieces, add water and boil until the vegetables are soft (about 20 minutes) then add salt and spices. On the first day of the diet people can eat all of the fruits except for bananas along with as much cabbage soup as they want.

Day 2. Soup and vegetables and a little bit of boiled potatoes are allowed. The vegetables can be fresh, boiled, or steamed.

Day 3 - Soup, fruit, and vegetables, but no potatoes.

Day 4 - A glass of fat free milk, 2 bananas, fruits, vegetables, and the cabbage soup.

Day 5 - 500 grams of boiled beef or skinless chicken or fish, soup, and tomatoes.

Day 6 - Green vegetables such as lettuce, meat, and of course cabbage soup.

Day 7 - Brown rice, vegetables, fruit juice (sugar free) and soup.

Repeat this for 31 days and you will see great changes.

BELOW SEE 10 HELPFUL HINTS.

1. Eat grains such as high fiber cereal, oatmeal, grits, etc. It is important to have a high fiber diet to keep the body cleansing regularly. Also, these carbohydrates start up your calorie burning machine. This is why fiber cereals are recommended for breakfast in most healthy eating plans.

2. Eat dark green leafy vegetables daily; such as; spinach, romaine lettuce, dark cabbage, kale and other greens. Dark vegetables are high in fiber and have many nutrients and vitamins that are needed for the body to function at a healthy level, and they are

low in calories. Because dark vegetables consist of a large percent of water you can indulge and still lose weight.

3. Eat at least 4 times each day, five when trying to lose weight. By eating often you won't have the opportunity to get hungry and overeat. Secondly, smaller meals are easier for the body to digest, burn off fat and unwanted calories. Because of how our bodies are designed, if you do not feed your body it will go into survival mode and hang onto extra weight versus releasing it.

4. Use portion control to lose weight. Never overeat. Put the appropriate portion of food on your plate. You have to know your portions, for example; steak or chicken should only be 4-5oz; most cooked carbs only 1/2 cup; fresh green vegetables, because they consist of a high percent of water, you can have 1 cup or more.

5. Read labels. They contain valuable information, such as: how many grams of sugar, sodium, carbs, calories, how much equals 1 serving, etc. Labels are your best friend. If you don't understand them it will be hard to lose weight.

6. Eat breakfast everyday. Breakfast is the most important meal of the day. When a healthy breakfast

is eaten it begins the calorie burning machine for the day. Whole grains and oatmeal are highly recommended because they get the metabolism working.

7. Eat fresh fruit but be selective on fruits eaten. Some fruits such as ripe bananas are extremely high in sugar and may be a detriment to your goals, but fruits like blueberries have antioxidants and help build your immune system and are low in calories.

8. Write down everything eaten in a journal. It is important to record everything that you eat. It allows you to see exactly what you are putting in your mouth all day long. It gives you better insight on why you may not be losing weight. You must record everything that you eat, what time and how much eaten.

9. Don't snack while watching TV. When you eat in front of the TV there may be very little connection on how much your mouth is taking in. This leads to overeating.

10. Don't eat empty calories. If you want to lose weight, make every calorie count. Some foods have great value, while others taste good but have no nutritional value and lots of calories. Know the difference

Balanced Three-Meal Two-Snack Plan

This meal plan is based on splitting daily calorie intake in three meals and two snacks. Mainly, lots of lean protein and veggies are loaded in this diet program.

Breakfast: For starting the day, half cup of egg whites, 1 apple, whole wheat toast and a tablespoon of butter or 2 tablespoons of peanut butter is enough.

Snack: For midday munching, 8 oz. of zero fat Greek yogurt, half cup of berries, 1 tablespoon of agave nectar or a protein bar (200 calories) are considered best.

Lunch: Lunch can include salad made with 3 cups spinach, 2 tablespoons full fat dressing and 4 oz. grilled chicken, along with a half cup garbanzo beans.

Dinner: For ending the day well, you can go for a baked salmon, half sweet potato, and 4 cups roasted vegetables cooked in 2 tablespoons olive oil.

The Vegan Plan

It is one of the latest diet plans, which is mainly popularized by a good number of celebrities. This diet program mainly involves cutting down the intake of processed foods to lose more weight. This plan does not obligate the dieters to stay hungry by cutting down the consumption. It simply replaces the processed food items with healthy ones.

Breakfast: One cup tofu (scrambled), two whole wheat bread slices, two wedges raw cantaloupe and one tablespoon of vegan margarine spread can start the day well.

 Snack: One table spoon flax seed in 4 oz. vanilla soy yogurt can serve the purpose.

Lunch: A perfect midday meal includes black bean and sweet potato salad with 2 oz. tofu for a protein kick.

Dinner: One cup quinoa (well cooked) and a single serving of grilled vegetables is suitable for ending the day well.

So, these are some simple and effective 30 day meal plans for getting back in shape easily.

CHAPTER FOUR

30 DAY MEAL PREP TO GET IN SHAPE

The most effective way is typically to continually get back to the fundamentals as well as making use of what works. Stick to good information and you should not follow the newest diets or even fads on losing weight and you're going to be fine. Now we will look into how nutrition along with what you take in may help you lose a substantial amount of unwanted weight.

What to eat

Water rich food items

Try eating plenty of water rich foods which includes vegetables along with fruit. Water rich foods are not just beneficial, they can be a very important factor in shedding weight. Any of these water rich foods are actually very much less dense and don't deliver a great deal of calories but while doing so continue to keep us feeling satisfied. Water will also help to flush out impurities which happen to be one of several vehicles that stick in to additional fat in our body. The easiest way to make this happen should be to have a side salad with each and every meal that you have and additionally switch out snacks such as sugars to fruit.

Antioxidants and vitamin rich foods

Foods containing more antioxidants would be a requirement to include in your diet plan should you want to lose weight. Nearly all food items that are rich in antioxidants are great for slimming down as they are lower in calories. Vitamins also help our bodies perform better. With the body staying at a proper level, it is usually far easier to get rid of fat since the body stream is much smoother and takes away harmful toxins easier.

Things to refrain from

Unhealthy fats

What's as vital as picking the right foods is understanding what to steer clear of. This is an obvious one: refrain from fatty foods. This is really important simply because fatty foods don't just store as fat on your body, but it makes you truly feel exhausted. Any time you feel really worn out you will find a higher chance you don't want to exercise as well. Unhealthy fats also block your system and therefore can make it more difficult for your body to cleanse and remove toxic compounds. These kinds of toxins keep hold of body fat and increases excess fat.

Sugar

Remember to keep far away from foods that have sugar. This includes candy, junk food, instant foods and more. Sugar is known as a supply of instant energy. The negative thing is if not burnt off, sugars can become extra fat and store in your body. Sugar is also high in calories and also low in nutrition. It is that which we call "empty calories". Foods which happen to be dense but are without any nutrients. Make sure you stick with purely natural sugars like fresh fruits rather than refined sugars which can do no good.

Since you now know exactly what to consume and just what not to consume, possibly the best way to lose more weight is generally to manage the portion you take in. Avoid overeating and you are on the right course. Even though it could be tough from time to time, the simplest way to accomplish this is to drink a big glass of water before you start to eat. This way, the body feels a bit more satiated just before you eat and it also helps clean out any toxic compounds which in turn helps to get rid of fat at the same time. A different way will be to save half your meal and eat it later. Eating a smaller amount but more often can help boost metabolism and this results in fat burning.

If you keep to the information above, you're going to be on the right track to creating your best physique. Reducing your weight isn't a difficult task and should not be overwhelming. Many weight loss trends help you to slim down but they do not keep us healthy and in most cases the excess weight returns. Maintaining everything we have discussed it will be better to keep the body weight away once you get going and also stay in an improved condition. Therefore, begin your journey now and please remember the principles of a healthier lifestyle.

Would you believe it if someone told you that eating certain foods could help you lose unwanted pounds? Naturally you wouldn't, but it is true that certain foods can help in reducing your weight. Imagine losing weight simply because you eat more of these particular foods. Without a doubt, all these fat burning foods should be included in your diet. If you eat these foods three times a day, and remain active; you will be amazed at the results.

1. Beans: These contain a ton of protein, carbs, and fiber. They give you the fuel that your body needs to work, not feel hungry, and ensure that your body is working like it should. As a result, it's important to add beans to your dietary plan.

2. Cinnamon: Research indicates that consuming as little as a quarter tablespoon of cinnamon will maintain healthy blood sugar levels and increase insulin production. You'll have more energy while craving less sweets. In the end you won't be burdened with extra pounds.

3. Fish: Fish reduces leptin, a fatty acid which is needed. Leptin will offset obesity and the slowing down of your metabolism. Also, eating fish increases levels of omega-3 acids, which can be instrumental in keeping your heart in good shape. Therefore, fish is great to include in your diet as a way to stay healthy and lose weight.

4. Berries and Apples: Certain fruits such as berries and apples contain the water-binding ingredient pectin. Eating fruits that contain a lot of pectin inhibits the absorption of fat and cholesterol. Therefore, keeping unwanted fat away will be a lot easier.

5. Garlic may smell funny but it's a star in boosting metabolism and aiding weight loss.

6. Ginger: Ginger is a vasodilator, meaning that it expands the body's blood vessels. This raises the body's metabolic level, aiding in weight loss.

7. Soybeans: These beans can be a fantastic way to consume protein that is low in fat. Amazingly, it maintains a low glycemic index and a stable sugar level, so you can eat sweet foods with no effects.

8. Green tea: Great tea is better for you than coffee. It can increase your metabolism from 28% to 77% while at the same time refreshing you. The greater amount you consume, the more of an effect you will observe in the rate of your metabolism.

Lose 20 lbs In Two Weeks

In 1995, WHO (World Health Organisation) estimated that 200 million adults and 18 million children under 5 years of age are obese. In 2000, it reported that this figure has increased to more than 300 million. Hectic lifestyles is the most blamed factor. Overweight people are much prone to heart diseases, high blood pressure, cholesterol levels, hypertension, cancer, arthritis, sleep apnea, strokes, brain damage and diabetes. Apart from this, obese people also develop low self-esteem and have appearance issues. They are looked upon as unhappy, unhealthy, tired, sick or lazy individuals. Losing weight increases self-esteem, induces the feel good factor and enhances the appearance, besides preventing major diseases.

Therefore, weight loss and fitness are issues of growing concern. People worldwide crave to shed their extra pounds and stay fit. Here we share with you some knowledge on how to lose 20 lbs in just two weeks. Of course, it takes a little bit effort on your part.

Dieting and exercising

Plan your diet. Say a big no to junk foods and carbonated drinks. Avoid all calorie rich foods. Calculate your calorie intake and restrict it to a certain level depending upon your energy requirements. Each and every single calorie counts when you are dieting.

Increase your metabolic rate, which is the rate at which your body processes and uses the food you eat. It is an easy and sensible technique to lose weight. Try taking several small meals a day instead of taking it in large amounts a few times a day. This burns your fats faster. Constant eating helps develop a higher metabolism within you in order to accommodate your frequent eating, hence burning calories fast.

Increase your physical activities, stay active, and include fibre rich diets to increase your metabolic rate. Including green tea in your daily fluid intake also helps in increasing your metabolism and energy level.

Go in for a detoxification of your system. It removes all the potentially harmful and toxic substances from your system and cleanses it. Follow a detox diet. Juice based detox diets are good options, especially, the lemonade diet. Detoxification helps you drop your liquid weight in a little time. Maintain a healthy lifestyle after detoxification.

Take eight glasses of water daily. Water plays an important role in weight loss by speeding up your metabolism and by ensuring proper digestion, besides rehydrating your body. Staying hydrated makes you feel more energetic, thus boosting your metabolic rate. Drinking water also reduces your strong craving for food.

Also, be sure to maintain your body's nutrition while dieting. Consume nutritious but low calorie food stuff. It is recommended that you cut 150-300 calories from your daily diet and burn 150-300 calories in exercising. Scientific studies say, dieting is the best method for weight loss. But in order to achieve effective weight loss, doing a combo of dieting and exercising is necessary.

You will have to spend an hour or more to achieve your desired goal of losing 20 lbs in 2 weeks. Exercising should be intensive and vigorous, instead of merely walking. Doing the same kind of work outs render it boring. To ensure that it is interesting, do a variety of activities like jogging, cycling, weight lifting, hiking, rowing, etc. Doing some abdominal crunches keeps in check the belly contours. Exercises, besides giving your desired weight loss, also ensure that you are in a good shape. It does more good too.

Have the right mind set

To get motivated and to stay motivated are two important facets of your mind settings that will help you in reaching your predetermined goal of getting rid of those 20 lbs.

"Many of life's failures are people who did not realize how close they were to success when they gave up" - Thomas Edison.

Motivation and perseverance are essentials that keep you in the right mind set to help you attain your dream come true body weight. Motivation is the conscious or subconscious driving force, which when combines with steady persistence makes you achieve your goal. It contributes to your thoughts and actions.

Reason away: Why do you want to lose weight? Is it to look better? To feel more confident? To walk that ramp? To get that attention from your crush? Or anything else? You state it. Reasoning helps you take the necessary action by fixing your attitude.

Here are some points that will help you stay motivated:

· Make up your mind that you will never quit.

· Stay focussed on the end result.

· Keep track of your successes.

· Keep your motivation on high levels.

The thing next in getting the right mind set is positive thinking. There is a dramatic power in positive thinking. Positive thinking is a mental attitude that anticipates and admits conducive conditions in all the spheres of life in terms of growth, expansion and success. It is expressed through one's words and actions.

CHAPTER FIVE

THE PRONS AND CONS OF LOW CARB DIET

Low carb diets are all the rage. They seem to work for many people, and these people swear by them. Unfortunately, they don't work for everyone who tries them. These people end up using an alternative method of weight loss. A low carbohydrate diet is basically cutting back or eliminating any foods which contain starches and carbohydrates and instead eating foods high in protein. For those who are curious about a low carb diet, you need to make sure it's right for you, your current health status, personal habits and lifestyle, and your ultimate goals.

With trying anything new, there are pros and cons to consider. And when it comes to dieting, you must be aware of all the issues related to your weight-loss and any weight-loss diet. The following gives you the "skinny" on the pros and cons in regards to low carbohydrate diets:

Pro - Because a low carbohydrate diet is all about eliminating carbs and not actual food, you can usually eat to your heart's content.

Con - Because you have to restrict yourself to certain foods, it can get monotonous.

Pro - Since low carb diets are so popular, you can find information about them quickly and easily.

Con - There is so much information about low carb diets it can get confusing and you still may not know everything you need to know before starting a low carb diet.

Pro - By eliminating foods high in carbs, you lose weight more quickly.

Con - When you eliminate certain food types, you also eliminate certain nutrients your body needs for optimal health.

Pro - It's easy to follow a low carb diet, the variety of foods can keep you satisfied.

Con - The foods you need to eat on a low carbohydrate diet can get expensive.

Pro - Low carb diets will get your cravings under control.

Con - You will go through withdrawals eating no or low carb foods only.

Pro - You will see faster weight loss when you eat low to no carbohydrate foods all the time.

Con - Low carb diets are harder to follow during special events, holidays and occasions when there are only high carb foods available.

Pro - Low carb diet are very effective for weight loss.

Con - To succeed on a low carbohydrate diet, you must have strong willpower.

Pro - Your immune system will improve with a low carbohydrate diet.

Con - Too many saturated fats are bad for the health of your heart.

Pro - You learn to eat healthier by ridding your body of carbs.

Con - Some carbs are not bad – complex carbs have nutritional value.

Pro - You will get high amounts of protein and can still enjoy eating the meats you love.

Con - People who are vegetarian will have trouble getting all the nutrition they need since they don't eat meat.

THE BASIC PRINCIPLE OF KETOGENIC DIET

One very popular weight loss program that many people are trying out are low carb diets. But are low carb diets really that effective?

To an extent, yes, low carb diets can make dieting a great deal easier. Typically, people using a low carb approach tend to have less hunger issues to deal with, tend to see reduced bloating, hence they look thinner, and also tend to enjoy the food since you're allowed to have more dietary fat with these approaches.

But, that said, there are some important things you must realize before starting up on a low carb diet. If you don't recognize these factors, you could wind up getting into quite a bit of trouble on a low carb diet and not see the types of results you're looking for.

Here's what you need to know about low carb diets.

Low Carb Diets and Exercise Carbs

First, it's going to be very important that you are having carb ups at some point during your exercise workout. This can be before or after the workout is finished, or in the form of one very large carb-up on the weekend. Doing so will help to ensure that the body has enough muscle glycogen storage to be able to continue on with the exercise programs you are asking it to perform.

Neglecting to take in carbs at this point can lead to feelings of fatigue and may even cause you to stop your fat loss workouts altogether.

Low Carb Diets Shouldn't Limit Vegetables

Next, you also want to be sure you're not limiting vegetables at all while on a low carb diet. Doing so would be very problematic because these are filled with plenty of vitamins, minerals, and antioxidants. Not too mention they are low in calories, high in fiber, and are one of the best diet foods to be eating.

So, don't limit your vegetable consumption even if you are on a low carb diet. You will want to watch out for the varieties that do contain more starch, such as peas, corn, and carrots, but otherwise you can eat quite a few without worry.

Low Carb Diets and Water Intake

Finally, the last thing to keep in mind is that low carb diets do tend to have a dehydrating effect on the body, therefore it's going to be very important that you make sure you're drinking plenty of liquids.

It would be a smart move to bump up your water intake slightly from what you'd normally drink – about 10-12 cups of fluid altogether should be plenty.

So, be sure you're keeping these points in mind when considering a low carb approach. While some people just do not feel well at all on low-carb diets, many others do have good success on them.

CHAPTER SIX

WHAT IS THE KETO DIET?

The keto diet involves going long spells on extremely low (no higher than 30g per day) to almost zero g per day of carbs and increasing your fats to a really high level (to the point where they may make up as much as 65% of your daily macronutrients intake.) The idea behind this is to get your body into a state of ketosis. In this state of ketosis the body is supposed to be more inclined to use fat for energy, and research says it does just this. Depleting your carbohydrate/ glycogen liver stores and then moving onto fat for fuel means you should end up shredded.

You then follow this basic platform from say Monday until Sat 12pm (afternoon) (or Sat 7pm, depending on whose version you read). Then from this time until 12 midnight Sunday night (so up to 36 hours later) you carb up.

(Some say, and this will also be dictated by your body type, that you can go nuts in the carb up and eat anything you want and then there are those that more wisely – in my view – prescribe still sticking to the clean carbs even during your carb up.)

So calculating your numbers is as simple as the following...

Calculate your required maintenance level of daily calories...

(if you are looking to drop quickly use 1300. I would not advise this, if you want a more level drop in body fat use 1500 and if you are going to actually attempt to maintain or possibly put on some lean muscle mass then use 1700)

Body weight in pounds x 15= a

Protein for the day 1g per body weight in pounds= b

Bx4=c (c= number of calories allotted to your daily protein allowance).

a-c= d (d= amount of calories to be allotted to fat intake).

D/9= g per day of fat to be consumed.

The end calculation should leave you with a very high number for your fat intake.

Now for those of you wondering about energy levels: Especially for training because there are no carbs, with there being such a high amount of fat in the diet you feel quite full and the fat is a very good fuel source for your body. One adaptation that I have made is to actually have a nice fish fillet about an hour before I train and I find it gives me enough energy to get through my workout. (I am aware of the arguments made to not have fats 2-3 hours either side of training. While I won't have fats 2-3 hours after training as I want quick absorption and blood flow, I see no issue with slowing everything down before training so my body has access to a slow digesting energy source).

There are some that say to have a 30g carb intake immediately after training – just enough to fill liver glycogen levels. And then there are those that say having even as much as that may push you out of ketosis, the state you are trying to maintain.

During my carb up period, for the sake of those who would like to know if you can get in shape and still eat the things you want (in moderation), for the first six weeks I will be relaxed about what I eat in this period but then the following 6 weeks I will only eat clean carbs.

I also like to make sure that the first workout of the week – as in a Monday morning workout – is a nice long full hour of work so I start cutting into the liver glycogen immediately.

KETOGENIC DIETS AND WEIGHT LOSS AND BODYBUILDING

A ketogenic diet is one where there are no carbs. Without carbohydrates the body burns fat as the primary fuel source. Since this is happening the body can tap into stored bodyfat for energy and we can end up leaner. While that is possible we need to look at what may happen.

For starters your energy will be drained. Without carbohydrates your body won't know what energy source to turn to for a few days so you may experience feelings of weakness while you train or until your body becomes adapted to using fat. While this isn't a bad thing you must understand that you have to change your training intensity. There's no way that you can keep training at a high intensity while you use one of these diets.

The next thing that you have to understand about using a ketogenic diet for weight loss or bodybuilding is that you need to eat more protein then normal. Since you don't have carbs, and carbs are protein sparing, you need to consume more protein so you don't lose muscle tissue. So make sure that you are eating at least six meals per day with a serving of protein coming every meal.

Then you have to make sure that you are getting enough fiber. Look to consume fiber from various sources such as green vegetables and fiber powder or pills like physillum husk. Now you need to add some healthily nutritional supplements since you want to make sure that you do your best to burn fat on these keto diets for weight loss and bodybuilding. First, make sure you consume healthy fats like omega-3 fish oils, cla, and gla. These fats will help to burn more body fat. Then you want to purchase a good branch chain amino acid powder as bcaas help to retain muscle mass and prevent muscle breakdown.

KETOGENIC DIETS FOR MANAGING TYPE 2 DIABETES

Ketogenic diets have been in use since 1924 in pediatrics as a treatment for epilepsy. A ketogenic (keto) diet is one that is high in fat and low in carbs. The design of the ketogenic diet is to shifts the body's metabolic fuel from burning carbohydrates to fats. With the keto diet, the body metabolizes fat, instead of sugar, into energy. Ketones are a byproduct of that process.

Over the years, ketogenic diets have been used to treat diabetes. One justification was that it treats diabetes at its root cause by lowering carbohydrate intake leading to lower blood sugar, which in turn, lowers the need for insulin which minimizes insulin resistance and associated metabolic syndrome. In this way, a ketogenic diet may improve blood glucose (sugar) levels while at the same time reducing the need for insulin. This point of view presents keto diets as a much safer and more effective plan than injecting insulin to counteract the consumption of high carbohydrate foods.

A keto diet is actually a very restrictive diet. In the classic keto diet for example, one gets about 80 percent of caloric requirements from fat and 20 percent from proteins and carbohydrates. This is a marked departure from the norm where the body runs on energy from sugar derived from carbohydrate digestion but by severely limiting carbohydrates, the body is forced to use fat instead.

A ketogenic diet requires healthy food intake from beneficial fats, such as coconut oil, grass-pastured butter, organic pastured eggs, avocado, fish such as salmon, cottage cheese, avocado, almond butter and raw nuts (raw pecans and macadamia). People on ketogenic diets avoid all bread, rice, potatoes, pasta, flour, starchy vegetables, and most dairy. The diet is low in vitamins, minerals, and nutrients and requires supplementation.

A low carbohydrate diet is frequently recommended for people with type 2 diabetes because carbohydrates turn to blood sugar which in large quantities cause blood sugar to spike. Thus, for a diabetic who already has high blood sugar, eating additional sugar-producing foods is like courting danger. By switching the focus from sugar to fat, some patients can experience reduced blood sugar.

Changing the body's primary energy source from carbohydrates to fat leaves behind the byproduct of fat metabolism, ketones in the blood. For some diabetic patients, this can be dangerous as a buildup of ketones may create a risk for developing diabetic ketoacidosis (DKA). DKA is a medical emergency requiring immediate medical attention. DKA signs include consistently high blood sugar, dry mouth, polyuria, nausea, breath that has a fruit-like odor and breathing difficulties. Complications can lead to a diabetic coma.

For many people, the ketogenic diet is a great option for weight loss. It is very different and allows the person on the diet to eat a diet that consists of foods that you may not expect.

When you eat a very low amount of carbs your body gets put into a state of ketosis. What this means is your body burns fat for energy. How low of an amount of carbs do you need to eat in order to get into ketosis? Well, it varies from person to person, but it is a safe bet to stay under 25g net carbs. Many would suggest that when you are in the "induction phase" which is when you are actually putting your body into ketosis, you should stay under 10g net carbs.

If you aren't sure what net carbs are, let me help you. Net carbs are the amount of carbs you eat minus the amount of dietary fiber. So if on the day you eat a total of 35g of net carbs and 13g of dietary fiber, your net carbs for the day would be 22. Simple enough, right?

So besides weight loss what else is good about keto? Well, many people talk about their improved mental clarity when on the diet. Another benefit is having an increase in energy. Yet another is a decreased appetite.

One thing to worry about when going on the ketogenic diet is something called "keto flu." Not everyone experiences this, but for those that do it can be tough. You will feel lethargic and you may have a headache. It won't last very long. When you feel this way make sure you get plenty of water and rest to get through it.

If this sounds like the kind of diet you would be interested in, then what are you waiting for? Dive head first into keto. You won't believe the results you get in such a short amount of time.

CHAPTER SEVEN

HOW TO ENSURE YOUR VEGAN MEALS AND RECIPES ARE LOW-CALORIE

Vegan Weight Loss Advice

Certain folk have trouble losing weight on the vegan lifestyle. Although the majority will experience weight loss on the vegan diet, there are always some who wonder what they are doing wrong. There are simple and easy measures that you can take to ensure that all of your vegan meals and recipes that you prepare are complementing your weight loss efforts.

1. Go steady with the oil

Olive oil and other healthy oils are essential for optimal health and will help keep your hair, skin and nails beautiful. However, because olive oil is a form of fat (the healthy type), it is very high in energy content. Therefore, to keep your vegan meals low-calorie you should measure out your olive oil with a spoon just as your recipes call for, rather than simply pouring the oil into your dish.

2. Keep an eye on your nut portions

Many vegan recipes feature walnuts, brazil nuts or other gourmet nuts to make the meal flavoursome and satisfying. If you are hoping to see some weight loss, however, only add nuts to one of your meals per day – not all three! This will help keep your diet low-calorie and low-fat and will ultimately result in a slimmer physique.

3. Don't eat too much vegan junk-food

You should endeavour to make your own wholesome vegan meals and recipes as often as you are able, rather than opting for quick vegan junk food. This will make you in control of your food, and you can make your vegan meals and recipes as low-calorie and low-fat as you please. Vegan junk food on the other hand is terrible for weight loss, with packet chips, cookies, chocolates, salty nuts and soft-drinks the main offenders. These foods are too high in energy to eat on a regular basis, so please stick to making your own fresh vegan meals to guarantee weight loss.

4. Share your vegan baking with your friends

There are so many beautiful and tasty vegan sweets and dessert recipes that you can make nowadays, and let's be fair, every vegan should enjoy their fair share. But when you do bake, only make one serving of the recipe rather than doubling or tripling it. Also, share your recipes with friends, family and colleagues to show a giving spirit and mostly to save yourself from unnecessary emotional eating.

You can take control of your calorie intake on the vegan diet to ensure a steady weight loss. Remember to go steady with the olive oil, keep an eye on you nut portions, limit your vegan junk-food and share your baking with friends. Making wise choices as such will help make your weight loss a sure success on the vegan diet.

VEGAN MEAL PLAN

Switching to a vegan diet can be a great way to lose weight and get healthier. A vegan does not eat any foods that contain or are made with animal products of any kind. This can be a restrictive lifestyle, but many people choose to make this change and it is no surprise with all the weight that can be lost. No matter if it is due to religious reasons, health reasons, or concern for animal welfare, a vegan diet can really change how you feel and how you look.

If you are thinking about making the move to a vegan lifestyle it might help for you to have a vegan meal plan. There are so many delicious options for vegan foods. This meal plan is just a jumping off point. It is a great idea to buy some vegan cookbooks. It is also great to check out the thousands of vegan recipes that are online. Be adventurous and try new things. Here are some vegan recipes for breakfast, lunch, dinner, and dessert.

Breakfast

• Scrambled Tofu

• 1 ½ tablespoon safflower oil

• 3 tablespoons diced onion

• 1 diced Serrano chili

• 1/2 teaspoon ground cumin

• 3 tablespoons chopped cilantro

• 20 oz tofu

• Salsa of your choosing

Instructions

Heat the oil; add in onion and sauté for 1 to 2 minutes. Add the chilies and cumin, cook for a few minutes. Crumble the tofu and cook, stirring frequently. Mix in the cilantro and season with salt. Serve with warm tortillas and salsa.

Lunch

- Sweet Corn Soup

- 6 ears of corn

- 1 tablespoon corn oil

- 1 small onion

- 1/2 cup grated celery root

- 7 cups water or vegetable stock

- Salt to taste

1. Shuck the corn and slice off the kernels.

2. In a large soup pot put in the oil, onion, celery root, and one cup of water. Let that mixture stew under low heat until the onion is soft.

3. Add the corn, salt and remaining water and bring it to a boil.

4. Cool briefly and then puree in a blender, then wait for it to cool

before putting it through a food mill.

5. Reheat and add salt and pepper to taste.

Dinner

Seared Portobello Mushrooms

• 1 large Portobello mushroom, stem removed

• Olive oil as needed

• Salt and pepper

• Shallot vinaigrette

1. Slice the mushroom into wide slices.

2. Brush both sides with oil and set them in the skillet over high heat. Sear for 4 to 5 minutes.

3. Once they start to brown remove them and place them on a platter with salt and pepper to taste.

4. Add vinaigrette to the top for flavor.

Lentil and Onion Croquettes

- 2 cups chopped yellow onion

- 2 tablespoons olive oil

- 1/2 cup finely chopped carrot

- 2 cups bread crumbs

- 1 cup lentils

- 3/4 cup celery chopped

- Salt and pepper

1. In a skillet over low heat cook the onion in the olive oil.

2. In a saucepan combine the lentils, celery, carrots, and salt covered with water. Bring this to a boil and then lower the heat to a simmer for about 30 minutes.

3. Drain the liquid. Puree the lentils until smooth.

4. Mix the lentils with the onion and bread crumbs. Season with salt and pepper.

5. Allow the mixture to cool and then form it into 3 inch rounds. Fry the

croquette balls in olive oil and set them on a paper towel to soak up the excess oil.

Dessert

Strawberry Ice

• 1 quart ripe strawberries

• Stevia (to taste)

1.   Pull out the core of the berries.

2.   Puree them in a food processor.

3.   Put stevia into a saucepan. Add half a cup of the puree into the stevia and heat stirring constantly until it is all dissolved.

4.   Add in the puree and freeze.

CHAPTER EIGHT

STAYING HEALTHY WITH VEGAN MEALS ON A KETO DIET

There are many reasons why people should be careful with what they eat. First off, they have too many activities to attend to every day. With each activity, their body consumes and burn energy. The environment is also no longer as safe as it was. Even the air that supplies the oxygen contains particles and bacteria that could cause diseases. One way to protect their body from diseases is by eating healthy and nutritious food.

Nowadays, people try to keep their bodies protected and healthy through exercise and healthy diets. Many people follow a vegetarian diet plan. However, even with this plan, people may still be at risk of some illnesses.

When a person prepares a meal, he has to remember that every ingredient he uses is special and is meant for something. Some ingredients are used to give the meal a pleasing taste. But most ingredients are used to infuse it with nutrients and vitamins that the body needs.

Meat, for example, is a good source of protein. Proteins act as the building blocks of the body. They are needed to develop the muscles, cartilages, and bones. Even skin and blood needs them. Without them, you may stay in the gym the whole day and obtain very little result. Going for high protein, low carb vegetarian foods is actually going to help you have stronger muscles and a leaner body.

Carbohydrate is another component that the human body needs. It is what keeps people doing what they have to do by helping them obtain energy. Unfortunately, having too much of it could lead to serious and long-term diseases like diabetes and high blood pressure. In fact, dieticians and other health experts recommend some low carb vegetarian recipes to people suffering from such conditions.

People who try to indulge in vegetarian meals without understanding how it works may deny their body some nutrients. That is because this diet may not include the sources of proteins, carbohydrates and some vitamins that are required by the body.

On the other hand, following a vegan meal may actually be a good start to a healthier lifestyle. But a person who intends to shift to this kind of diet should first look at what he needs. He must consider his activities and health conditions. He needs to determine what he actually wants to develop or remove from his body. Taking these things into consideration would help him obtain faster results, and a fitter and healthier body. Most importantly, it would help him determine what vegetarian diet plan to follow.

On the vegan diet you should experience a profound detoxification of your body, a restoral of your health, a newfound zest for life, and of course, weight loss. Most folk who go on the vegan diet will lose weight, but there are the minority who do not. What are they doing wrong? Let's look at several mistakes that they may be making which are greatly sabotaging their weight loss efforts.

1. Over-eating

All foods should be eaten in moderation – regardless of how healthy they are. For example, one single banana is low in calories (approximately 100). Most vegans love bananas and will happily consume two or three a day. But what if you had 10 bananas in one day plus your other meals? This means that you will be consuming 1000 calories per day with bananas alone. This may sound like a crazy example, but I'm sure it gets the point across. You should eat all foods in moderation. Eat generous sized meals but don't make yourself sick. Eat your meals with intuition, balance and self-control. This will ensure that you will lose weight on the vegan diet.

2. Too many Nuts

Nuts are an essential food for those on the vegan diet due to their high nutritional properties, particularly for their protein and healthy-fat content. But the problem is when you have too many as the calories add up fast. Many folk say that they can easily polish off an entire container of nuts in one sitting. I'm sorry to say this, but if you intend to lose weight on the vegan diet, you need to limit your serving of nuts. Don't deprive yourself of them, but one or two handfuls per day should be sufficient.

3. Too much oil

Olive oil and other healthy oils are very good for your hair, skin and nails and you should consume a couple of tablespoons every day. But these oils are also very high in calorie content so please measure out your servings with a spoon, rather than happily pour the oil into your dish like a free-spirited chef. Just remember, by sensibly measuring out your olive oil you can keep your vegan meals low-calorie and low-fat. This will in turn help you to lose weight.

4. Too many avocadoes

Avocadoes are considered one of the top superfoods in the world. Due to their super-high nutrient content, they can help boost your health and make you beautiful on the inside and outside. But they are also high in energy due to their healthy fat content, so please stick to half to one medium sized avocado per day. Limiting your avocado portions will help ensure that your vegan meals will be low-fat and low-calorie.

5. Vegan Junk-Food

Nobody should eat much junk food, whether vegan or not. The vegan junk food list is long, with the common rogues being packet chips, biscuits, chocolate, lollies and soft-drinks. So stay away from these foods most of the time and only have these on special occasions. It's all about eating in moderation. Eat this food only a couple of times per week rather than on a daily basis.

These are the most common causes why some vegans cannot lose weight. Really, the key is to enjoy your vegan food in moderation, limit your portion of nuts, oils and avocadoes, and steer away from vegan junk food.

Benefits of a Vegan Lifestyle

One common notion about becoming a vegan is that you'll miss foods that are not part of the diet, such as meat. However, most people who begin following a plant-based diet come to find it expansive and empowering instead of restrictive. The truth is you will eat better than you did in the past and feel better as well. Cravings for meat, fish, and dairy products will dissipate over time until they are not missed. If you are thinking about becoming a vegan, below are six benefits of the lifestyle that may help your decision.

Deeper Compassion

A vegan's compassion extends its reach to all living creatures. With increased compassion comes greater acceptance of all life and the appreciation that it adds value to our own, making us stronger.

Expanded Palate

Vegans learn to enjoy a very wide range of vegetables which leads to an expanded palate. Recipes abound for cooking every vegetable imaginable. When veggies are just a side dish, it's convenient to settle for a few of them to complement meat, such as potato salad, peas and carrots, or corn. Once veggies are the main dish, however, one starts to appreciate many more ingredients enriching the dining experience.

Global Impact

The vegan lifestyle is much more than food. It's about the environment, climate, sustainable development, efficient allocation of food sources, and animal welfare. Many of the themes associated with going green are linked to veganism. When one chooses to be a vegan, one participates and supports these themes. The impact of eating vegan is so powerful, that if everyone did it constantly or even occasionally, many of these issues would resolve themselves.

Increased Mobility

Nutritionists, dietitians, and health scientists are confirming the health benefits of a plant-based diet over a meat-based one. Lower blood pressure, reduced risk of heart disease and cancer, and longer life spans are possible outcomes of a vegan diet. Fewer health problems mean that one is more active and mobile and can enjoy life more fully.

Larger Social Network

The vegan community is large and growing. Vegans enjoy sharing their experiences and finding companions who understand the reasons for their eating habits. Meeting and connecting with new people is one of the fun social aspects of being vegan.

New Knowledge

The vegan diet is focused on ingredients, health, and nutrition. To enjoy vegan food and stay healthy, one inevitably learns more about nutrition and the impact of ingredients on health. Over time, by paying attention to what it consumed and the value of each ingredient, one becomes familiar with vitamins, minerals, protein, fiber, antioxidants, and phytonutrients and with it comes new knowledge and power.

The benefits of a vegan lifestyle make one a more empowered person. New experiences lead to new ideas and new ways to enjoy and fully appreciate life. Try eating more vegan meals and enjoy the positive impact.

CHAPTER NINE

HOW TO FOLLOW A PLANT-BASED KETOGENIC DIET

So how exactly do you slip into ketosis without loading up on butter and bacon? And how can you ensure that your nutrient needs are still being met while following a plant-based ketogenic diet?

The key is to swap out your starchy veggies for low-carb alternatives while also filling your diet with plenty of plant-based fats and proteins. This can help you stay under your carbohydrate goal and provide your body with the important vitamins and minerals that it needs to stay healthy.

High-carb foods that should be limited in your diet include:

• High-Sugar Fruits (apples, oranges, bananas, grapes, etc.)

• Starchy vegetables (potatoes, sweet potatoes, winter squash, peas, corn, etc.)

• Sugar (including honey, maple syrup, agave syrup, etc.)

• Legumes (beans, lentils, peas, etc.)

• Grains (wheat products, rice, quinoa, cereal, etc.)

Instead, be sure to include plenty of nutrient-rich, low-carb plant-based foods in your diet, such as:

• Fermented foods (tempeh, natto, etc.)

• Leafy greens (kale, chard, spinach, collard greens, etc.)

• Non-starchy vegetables (asparagus, carrots, cauliflower, onions, mushrooms, peppers, etc.)

• Nuts (almonds, walnuts, pistachios, pecans, etc.)

• Seeds (chia seeds, flax seeds, hemp seeds, pumpkin seeds, etc.)

• Low sugar fruits (blackberries, raspberries, strawberries, etc.)

• Healthy fats (coconut oil, MCT oil, olive oil)

Including enough protein in your diet can be challenging on any plant-based diet, let alone a plant-based ketogenic diet. Fortunately, there are tons of healthy options that can provide the protein you need to keep you going.

A few examples of low-carb, plant-based proteins include:

• Tempeh

• Natto

• Nutritional Yeast

• Spirulina

• Nuts

• Seeds

High-quality, low-sugar plant-based protein powders

Similarly, nixing all dairy products from your diet can make it tricky to get in enough fat, but there are plenty of plant-based sources of fat available that can help you easily meet your needs.

Some of the healthiest plant-based fats include:

• Avocado Oil

• Coconut Oil

• Olive Oil

- MCT Oil

- Avocado

- Nuts

- Seeds

Note that you can easily swap these nutritious foods into your favorite recipes to make them completely plant-based and keto-friendly. Nutritional yeast, for example, makes a great substitute for cheese while tempeh can be crumbled and cooked like ground beef to make delicious veggie tacos or lettuce wraps.

Sample Meal Plan:

Wondering what exactly a plant-based ketogenic diet looks like? Here's a one-day sample meal plan that you can follow to help get you started!

Breakfast:

Gluten-free oatmeal (2 grams net carbs per serving)

Lunch:

Baked tempeh (3 grams net carbs per serving)

Cauliflower tabbouleh salad (6 grams net carbs per serving)

Olive oil vinaigrette (0 grams net carbs per serving)

Dinner:

Raw walnut tacos (4 grams net carbs per serving)

Super cilantro guacamole (5 grams net carbs per serving)

Snacks:

Keto smoothie with avocado, chia seeds & cacao (6.5 grams net carbs)

Almonds (2.5 grams net carbs per 1-oz serving)

Spicy roasted pumpkin seeds (10 grams carbs per 1-oz serving)

Daily Total: 39 grams net carbs

WHAT VEGASs EAT IN THEIR KETO JOURNEY

But can a vegetarian or vegan be Keto? Does the necessity of fat and the small margin for carbs eliminate anyone else except meat and dairy consumers? No. The vegetarian and vegan can still be LCHF while observing their food preferences. Here at Keys to Ketosis, we've provided a vegan ketogenic diet food list to help anyone who is conscious of what types of food they consume, but still wants to (or has to) pursue a low-carb, high-fat lifestyle.

Check out the list of compiled low-carb vegan diet below!

Tofu

The point of tension for a vegan/vegetarian attempting to pursue a LCHF will be the choices for a base food or "main course" food that will provide much of their protein and fat sources.

On the vegan ketogenic diet food list, tofu will be one of the big operators for finding interesting ways to creating mindful food that also assists you in your low-carb pursuit. Tofu is a versatile food, that comes in various forms and can be cooked in a variety of ways, including grilling, frying, baking, or just eating it raw. Having this on your vegan ketogenic diet food list will be imperative to maintaining excitement and variety.

Tofu Nutriton Facts (1/2 Cup):

Calories: 94

Fats: 6g

Carbs: 2.3g

Protein: 10g

Nuts

Nuts are a must on the Ketogenic diet, but peanuts should be eaten judiciously, due to their classification of legume, which means they belong to the same family as beans, and share their high carb profiles. However, you can use peanut butter for a topping, but once again, not in excess.

The good news for your vegan ketogenic diet food list is that there are plenty of nuts that are permissible – and beneficial – to being low-carb high-fat.

The best of the best include the following (in descending order from best to worst):

- Almonds

- Macadamia Nuts

- Walnuts

- Pecans

- Cashews and Pistachios

Nut based flours can also be used for baking instead of high-carb wheat flour.

MCT Oil

MCT Oil will make staying LCHF on a vegan diet easier than it has ever been.

MCT oil for keto diet plan

By using this supplement in shakes, as a dressing, or on other foods, you can ensure that your body is getting the correct doses of fatty acids that are essential to ketosis.

Other ideas:

Mixing in toppings (like mayo)

Use while baking food instead of regular baking oil

The great thing about using MCT Oil (and other exogenous ketones) is that you can counterbalance some of the carbs you will inevitably take by adhering to the vegan ketogenic diet food list.

Olive and Coconut Oil

Other oils that are great for toppings or cooking are coconut and olive oil. Both of these oils provide a great source of healthy fats, and a broad range of uses for food.

And unlike MCT Oil, these oils can be used for frying and sautéing food. Coconut oil is more stable than olive oil, so it is the better choice for using at high temperatures.

The benefit that these two oils bring to your vegan ketogenic diet food list, is their ability to provide vibrancy with flavor. While MCT Oil can provide a more potent shot of healthy fat, it can also bring with it a taste that can be hard to handle if not masked, whereas coconut and olive oil are both pleasurable to consume.

Greens

Since fruits are a no-no on the ketogenic diet (except for avocados), you will need to be strategic about eating enough greens to get the nutrients you'd get from the fruits you'd normally consume on a standard vegan diet.

The vegetables that you should keep stocked on your ketogenic diet food list are leafy greens like kale, collard greens, spinach, swiss chard, and others of the same family.

These vegetables, mixed with avocados and keto friendly oils (listed above) will help you stay vibrant from proper vitamin intake, while also helping you maintain a low-carb lifestyle.

Fatty Produce (Avocado)

The avocado is the hallmark of healthy fats from fruits (yes, avocados are a fruit). It is also capable of being used in every meal of the day, pairing well with salads. Did we mention that guacamole is incredible?

Avocados are considered a superfood, because of the research that suggests they help lower cholesterol, and even ward off cancer!

Nutrition Info (1 avocado):

Calories: 322

Fats: 29g

Carbs: 17g

Protein: 4g

CONCLUSION

What does it mean to be on a keto meal (often shortened to "keto") diet? When you're on a keto diet, you consume a very low-carb, high-fat diet. The idea behind this way of eating and why it can work so well is that when the body gets such small amounts of glucose from carbohydrates, it can burn another fuel source — fat — for energy. This is why the keto diet is known for helping the body to burn fat impressively fast! What if you're not trying to lower the number on your scale? The keto diet still may appeal to you since by limiting sugars and processed grains, you may lower your risk of developing type 2 diabetes, a disease which is becoming more and more common these days.

KETO MEAL PREP FOR BEGINNERS

INTRODUCTION

When the average person eats a meal rich in carbs, their body takes those carbs and converts them into glucose for fuel. Glucose is the body's main source of fuel when carbs are present in the body; on a Keto diet, there are very low if any at all carbs consumed, which forces the body to utilize other forms of energy to keep it functioning properly. This is where healthy fats come into play; with the absence of carbs, the liver takes fatty acids in the body and converts them into ketone bodies.

The ketogenic diet, or keto, is a diet that consists of very low carbs and high fat. That may sound too good to be true for many. Well, on this diet, this is a great day of eating and you can follow the rules perfectly with that meal plan.

A keto diet causes ketone bodies to be produced by the liver and shifts the body's metabolism away from glucose in favor of fat-burning. A ketogenic diet restricts carbohydrates below a certain level (generally 100 per day). The ultimate determinant of whether a diet is ketogenic or not is the presence or absence of carbohydrates. Protein and fat intake vary. Contrary to popular belief, eating fat is not what causes ketosis. In the past, starvation diets were used often to induce ketosis

A lack of carbohydrates or presence of them ultimately determines if the diet is ketogenic.

In most eating plans, the body runs on a mixture of protein, fats, and carbohydrates. When carbohydrates are severely restricted and glycogen storage (glucose in muscle and liver) is depleted, the body begins to utilize other means to provide energy. FFA (free fatty acids) can be used to provide energy, but the brain and nervous system are unable to use FFA's. Although the brain can use ketone bodies for energy.

Ketone bodies are by products of incomplete FFA breakdown in the liver. Once they begin to accumulate fast and reach a certain level, they are released, accumulated in the bloodstream, and cause a state called ketosis. As this occurs, there is a decrease in glucose production and utilization. There is also less reliance on protein to meet energy requirements by the body. Ketogenic diets are often referred to as protein sparing, as they help to spare LBM while dropping body fat.

In regards to ketogenic diets, there are two primary hormones-insulin, glucagon that need to be considered. Insulin can be described as a storage hormone as its job is to take nutrients out of the bloodstream and carry them to target tissues. Insulin carries glucose from the blood to the liver and muscles, and it carries FFA from the blood into adipose tissue (stored fat triglyceride). On the other hand, glucagon breaks down glycogen stores (especially in the liver) and releases them into the blood.

When carbs are restricted or removed, insulin levels drop while glucagon levels rise. This causes an enhanced FFA release from fat cells, and increased FFA burning in the liver. This accelerated burning of FFA in the liver is what leads to ketosis. There are a number of other hormones involved with this process as well.

CHAPTER ONE

KETO MEAL PREPARATION

Obesity rates have skyrocketed; the incidence of diabetes has also increased, the main reason being that people's diets consist mainly of carbohydrates and fats, and the two don't mix well together; but protein and fats do mix well together. Watching your intake of carbohydrates is very important for weight loss. Low-carb diets or diets that teach food combining are very effective in weight loss. Ok, now for the myths.

The truth is that the father of low-carb, high-protein dates back to 1863, William Banting of England, who wrote a little booklet titled "Letter on Corpulence Addressed to the Public", William Banting is considered the father of low-carbohydrate dieting. He proved this over years, helping people lose weight without any side-effects.

The myth says that a low-carb, high-protein, and high-fat diet raises cholesterol; the truth is it actually lowers cholesterol.For one year, researchers at the Veterans Affairs Medical Center in Philadelphia followed 132 obese adults randomized into two groups. One restricted carbohydrate intake to less than 30 grams per day (low-carbohydrate diet); the other restricted caloric intake by 500 calories, with 30% of calories from fat (conventional diet).83% percent of the study group had diabetes or other risk factors for heart disease.

In the low-carb group, triglyceride levels decreased more and HDL ('good') cholesterol levels decreased less than in the low-fat group (high levels of triglycerides, a fat in the blood, are associated with heart disease). People with diabetes on the low-carb diet had a better control of blood sugar.

The low-carbohydrate group had more beneficial changes in triglyceride levels and HDL cholesterol levels than the low-fat diet group; the low-carb diet group also contained vitamins and other nutritional supplements.

Another myth says that a low-carb diet will raise your blood pressure; the truth is, with lower LDL levels and VLDL levels, blood pressure levels drop.

If people have high blood pressure and a weight problem, a low-carbohydrate diet might be a better option than a weight-loss medication.

Another myth says that you need carbohydrates or glucose for brain function; the truth is if you are on a hardcore low-carb, high-protein diet, where carbohydrates are non-existent, you are on what is called a Ketogenic Diet. When on such a strict diet, your body produces ketones in the absence of carbohydrates, then converts the ketones into a form of glucose that enables proper brain function.

Will I gain all my weight back if I stop my low-carb diet? That is totally false, it does not matter what diet you choose, if you are successful in your weight loss and then stop your diet, 9 out of 10 times you revert back to your old eating habits, and start eating junk and over-indulge, then of course you gain the weight back.

-Another myth: eating protein makes you fat. This is totally false; protein actually raises your calorie-burning metabolism by as much as 30% over carbohydrates. When proteins are consumed, your body must digest and break them down into amino acids, this takes energy and plenty of it, this actually helps you lose weight; not gain it.

Another myth: high protein diets include fats, and fats are bad for me. Fats in the absence of carbohydrates burn more efficiently, and do not clog your arteries. As the studies show LDL's (low density lipoproteins) which are the artery cloggers, are lowered. The HDL's, which are the good carbohydrates, are raised even though your fat intake is increased, that, as mentioned above is attributed to low-carb intake. Carbs and fat don't mix, your body cannot efficiently break them down together, your liver is over-burdened and ends up converting the carbohydrates into fat, unless of course you are exercising like crazy.

Anotyher myth states: I will not have any energy with the low-carb diet. This is totally false, unless you are a marathon runner or bodybuilder. When you consume small amounts of carbohydrates, your body needs another source of energy; when glycogen levels are gone, your body starts using fat for energy and combustion. If you are extremely active, then it will take about 2-3 weeks, after that, your body is acclimated to your new eating habits and adjusts, energizing you as before. If you are involved in a endurance sport, then of course you need extra carbs to be competitive. If you are an athlete or work-out extensively, then you probably would not be dieting anyway, and a low-carb high-protein is a mute point.

Here are the most common myths associated to the low-carb diet plan.

1. It has been said that the low-carb diet will reduce the amount of calcium in your body. This couldn't be

farther from the truth, as since the low-carb diet is rich in protein, this, in fact actually prevents calcium from entering your urine.

2. They say the low-carb diet plan will damage one's kidneys. Not unless one already has a kidney defect, because with the low-carb diet, though rich in protein, this is not what the entire meal is made of. Once on a low-carb diet, one still must observe the balancing of the meals consumed. It has been said that some doctors actually recommend a low-carb diet for some of their patients in order to treat kidney problems.

3. Moving from the kidneys, there's also this myth that while on a low-carb diet, you're dicing with heart disease. On the contrary, it's a fact that a low-carb diet plan actually reduces the risk of having heart disease. It has also been proven that even foods containing lots of animal fat and proteins do not constitute risk for heart disease.

4. There is no fibre present in the low-carb diet. The low carb diet is, on the contrary, full of fibre, and research also shows that the presence of this fibre actually lessens the effect and the amount of carbohydrates in one's body. Which makes the low-carb diet a very pragmatic diet plan.

5. While on a low-carb diet, you're not allowed to consume fruits or vegetables. This is not true, because it's not a secret that the population for one reason or another just do not like eating fruits and vegetables. This goes back for years, and governments all over the world are now making it a point of duty by recommending the daily intakes. So, just because people have preferences doesn't mean it's down to the low-carb diet plan.

6. A low carb-diet means total elimination of carbohydrates. Even the most critical doctors, scientists, or nutritionists will dispel this, as in any given meal, one must have at least 45% - 65% carbohydrates in their meals, depending on each individual, of course.

7. Low-carb diets will produce permanent bad breath. This to some extent is true, but not because you're on a low-carb diet plan. This is simply because, people, regardless of what weight-loss or diet program they embark on, feel they have to abstain from other meals, such as eating fruits and vegetables. Even if one's not on any form of diet, not eating fruits and vegetables will certainly attract bad breath. To combat this is simple, just eat more fruits and vegetables on a daily basis. This has nothing to do with a low-carb diet alone!

I hope with the above explanations, you can now take the plunge with ease and confidence and start embarking on a new and healthy journey and lifestyle using the low-carb diet plan.

Don't Be Confused About Low-Carb Diets

The high amounts of carbohydrates in our diet has led to increasing problems with obesity, diabetes, and other health problems. Critics, on the other hand, attribute obesity and related health problems to over-consumption of calories from any source, and lack of physical activity. Critics also express concern that the lack of grains, fruits, and vegetables in low-carbohydrate diets may lead to deficiencies of some key nutrients, including fiber, vitamin C, folic acid, and several minerals.

Any diet, whether low or high in carbohydrates, can produce significant weight-loss during the initial stages of the diet. But remember, the key to successful dieting is in being able to lose the weight permanently

- Differences Between Low-Carb Diets

There are many popular diets designed to lower carbohydrate consumption. Reducing total carbohydrates in the diet means that protein and fat will represent a proportionately greater amount of the total caloric intake.

The weight loss on low-carb diets is a function of caloric restriction and diet duration, and not reduced carbohydrate intake. This finding suggests that if you want to lose weight, you should eat fewer calories and do so over a long time period.

Little evidence exists on the long-range safety of low-carb diets. Despite the medical community's concerns, no short-term adverse effects have been found on cholesterol, glucose, insulin, and blood-pressure levels among participants on the diets. But, adverse effects may not show up because of the short period of the studies. Researchers note that losing weight typically leads to an improvement in these levels anyway, and this may offset an increase caused by a high-fat diet. The long-range weight change for low-carb and other types of diets is similar.

Low-carb diets do not enable the consumption of more calories than other kinds of diets, as has been often reported. A calorie is a calorie and it doesn't matter whether they come from carbohydrates or fat. Study discrepancies are likely the result of uncontrolled circumstances; i.e. diet participants that cheat on calorie consumption, calories burned during exercise, or any number of other factors. The drop-out rate for strict (i.e. less than 40 grams of CHO/day) low-carb diets is relatively high.

What Should You Do? - There are 3 important points I would like to re-emphasize:

- The long-range success rate for low-carb and other types of diets is similar.

- Despite their popularity, little information exists on the long-term efficacy and safety of low-carbohydrate diets.

- Strict low-carb diets are usually not sustainable as a normal way of eating. Boredom usually overcomes willpower.

The diet you choose should be a blueprint for a lifetime of better eating, not just a quick weight-loss plan to reach your weight goal. If you can't see yourself eating the prescribed foods longer than a few days or a week, then chances are it's not the right diet. To this end, following a moderately low-fat diet with a healthy balance of fat, protein, carbohydrates, and other nutrients is beneficial.

If you do decide to follow a low-carb plan, remember that certain dietary fats are associated with reduction of disease. Foods high in unsaturated fats that are free of trans-fatty acids such as olive oil, fish, flaxseeds, and nuts are preferred to fats from animal origins.

Another alternative to "strict" low-carb dieting would be to give up some of the bad carbohydrate foods but not "throw out the baby with the bath water". In other words, foods high in processed sugar, snacks, and white bread would be avoided, but foods high in complex carbohydrates such as fruit, potatoes, and whole grains, retained.

1. SESAME BROILED CHICKEN

Prep time: 5 minutes
Cook time: 20 minutes
Total time: 25 minutes

Ingredients:
4 bone-in, skin-on chicken thighs
¼ teaspoon salt
¼ teaspoon freshly ground black pepper
2 tablespoons soy sauce
2 tablespoons sugar-free maple syrup
1 tablespoon sesame oil
1 teaspoon minced garlic
1 teaspoon red wine vinegar
½ teaspoon crushed red pepper flakes

Direction:
Season the chicken with the salt and pepper. Set aside.
In a bowl large enough to hold the chicken, combine the soy sauce, maple syrup, sesame oil, garlic, vinegar, and red pepper flakes. Reserve about one quarter of the sauce.
Add the chicken thighs to the bowl, skin-side up. Submerge in the soy sauce. Refrigerate to marinate for at least 15 minutes.
Preheat the oven to broil.

Remove the chicken from the refrigerator. Place the thighs skin-side down in the baking dish.

Place the dish in the preheated oven, about six inches from the broiler. Broil for 5 to 6 minutes with the oven door slightly ajar. Turn the chicken skin-side up. Broil for about 2 minutes more.

Turn the chicken again so it is now skin-side down. Move the baking dish to the bottom rack of the oven. Close the oven door and broil for another 6 to 8 minutes.

Turn the chicken again to skin-side up. Baste with the reserved sauce. Close the oven door and broil for 2 minutes more.

Remove the chicken from the oven. With a meat thermometer, check the internal temperature.It should reach at least 165°F.

Cool the chicken for 5 minutes before serving.

2. GREEK EGG BAKE

Prep time: 5 minutes
Cook time: 25 minutes
Total time: 30 minutes

Ingredients:
12 eggs
1 cup kale, chopped
1/4 cup sun-dried tomatoes
1/2 cup feta
1/2 tsp oregano
Salt and pepper to taste
Greek egg bake recipe

Directions:
Pre-heat the oven to 350 degrees.
Whisk together eggs.
Add in kale, tomaotes, feta, and spice.
Line a baking pan with foil (makes it easier to remove from the pan).
Spray with non-stick spray.
Bake in the oven for about 25 minutes.
Slice and serve...or portion out for the week. Will keep in the fridge for 4-5 days.

3. TURMERIC SCRAMBLED EGG

Prep Time: 5 minutes

Cook time: 6 minutes

Ingredients:

4 large eggs

2 Tbsp. milk of choice

2 Tsp. dried turmeric

½ Tsp. dried parsley

salt& black pepper to taste

steamed veggie of choice

pre-cooked sausage of choice

turmeric eggs, broccoli, and sausage

Directions:

Spray a small frying pan with nonstick cooking spray and bring to a medium heat.

In a small bowl, whisk together the eggs, milk, turmeric, parsley, salt and pepper.

Transfer the eggs to the heated pan. Cook 2-3 minutes stirring constantly to break them apart.

Flip the eggs and cook another 2-3 minutes, or until desired.

Transfer the eggs to two meal prep containers, diving them evenly. Add steamed vegetables and sausage!

4. CAULIFLOWER HASH BROWNS

Prep time: 20 minutes
Cook time: 15 minutes
Total time: 45 minutes

Ingredients:
1 small head grated cauliflower (about 3 cups)
1 large egg
3/4 cup shredded cheddar cheese
1/4 tsp cayenne pepper (optional)
1/4 tsp garlic powder
1/2 tsp pink salt
1/8 tsp black pepper

Directions:
Grate entire head of cauliflower.
Microwave for 3 minutes and let cool. Place in paper towels or cheese cloth and wring out all the excess water.
Place wrung out cauliflower in a bowl, add rest of ingredients and combine well.
Form into six square shaped hash browns on a greased baking tray.
Place in a 400° oven for 15-20 minutes.
Let cool for 10 minutes and hash browns will firm up.
Serve warm. Enjoy!

5. BLUEBERRY PANCAKE BITES

Prep time: 15 minutes
Cook time: 25 minutes
Total time: 40 minutes

Ingredients:
4 large eggs
1/4 cup Swerve sweetener
1/2 tsp vanilla extract
1/2 cup [url]coconut flour
1/4 cup butter, melted
1 tsp baking powder
1/2 tsp salt
1/4 tsp cinnamon
1/3 to 1/2 cup water
1/2 cup Wyman's frozen wild blueberries

Directions:
Preheat oven to 325 F and grease a mini muffin tin (24 cavity) very well (double grease, first with butter and then with coconut oil spray).
In a blender combine the eggs, sweetener, and vanilla extract.Blend until smooth.
Add the coconut flour, melted butter, baking powder, salt, and cinnamon. Blend again until smooth. It will seem very liquidy but let it sit a few minutes and it will thicken up considerably. Add 1/3 cup of the water

and blend again. If it's still very thick, add a little additional water. You shouldn't be able to pour it, but you should be able to scoop it out of the blender easily.

Divide among the prepared muffin cups. Add a few blueberries to each. Press them gently into the batter. Bake 20 to 25 minutes, until set. Let cool a few minutes in the pan and then serve with your favourite low carb pancake syrup.

6. KETO BAGELS

Prep time: 15 minutes
Cook time: 14 minutes

Ingredients:
2 cups almond flour
1 tbsp baking powder
1 tsp garlic powder
1 tsp onion powder
1 tsp dried Italian seasoning
3 large eggs, divided
3 cups shredded low moisture mozzarella cheese
5 tbsp cream cheese
3 tbsp Everything Bagel Seasoning

Directions:
Preheat oven to 425°.Line a rimmed baking sheet with parchment paper or a Silpat.

In a medium mixing bowl, combine the almond flour, baking powder, garlic powder, onion powder, and dried Italian seasoning. Mix until well combined, put the mixture through a flour sifter to ensure that all the baking powder gets mixed in with the rest of the ingredients.

Crack one of the eggs into a small bowl and fork whisk. This will be the egg wash for the top of the bagels. The other two eggs will go in the dough.

In a large microwave safe mixing bowl, combine the mozzarella cheese and cream cheese. Microwave for 1 minute and 30 seconds. Remove from microwave and stir to combine. Return to microwave for 1 additional minute. Mix until well combined.

To the mixing bowl, add the remaining 2 eggs and the almond flour mixture. Mix until all ingredients are well incorporated. If the dough gets too stringy and unworkable, simply put it back in the microwave for 30 seconds to soften and continue mixing.

Divide the dough into 6 equal portions.Roll each portion into a ball.

Gently press your finger into the center of each dough ball to form a ring. Stretch the ring to make a small hole in the center and form it into a bagel shape.

Brush the top of each bagel with the egg wash.

Top each bagel with Everything Bagel Seasoning.

Bake on the middle rack for 12-14 minutes or until golden brown.

7. LOW-CARB BREAKFAST PIZZA

Prep time: 10 minutes
Cook time: 30 minutes
Total time: 40 minutes

Ingredients:
12 eggs
1/2 cup heavy cream
1/2 tsp salt
1/4 tsp pepper
8 oz sausage
2 cups peppers, sliced
1 cup cheese, shredded

Directions:
Preheat oven to 350°.
Add peppers to microwave for 3 minutes.
Brown sausage in cast iron skillet.
Take out and set aside.
Mix eggs, cream, salt and pepper together and add to skillet.
Cook for 5 minutes until the sides start to set up.
Add to oven and bake for 15 minutes.
Take out and add sausage, peppers and cheese.
Set under broiler for 3 minutes.

8. KETO BACON SAUSAGE MEATBALLS

Prep time: 10 minutes
Cook time: 30 minutes

Ingredients:
1 pound spicy italian sausage whole 30, if needed
9 sliced sugar-free bacon
2 tbsp garlic, minced
2 tbsp white onion diced
1 tbsp dried oregano

Directions:
Preheat oven to 375 F. Prepare a standard muffin pan by greasing 9 cavities lightly with coconut oil.
In a large mixing bowl, combine the Italian sausage, garlic, onion and oregano.
Roll the mixture into 9 equal balls with your hands and place on a plate.
Wrap each ball with a slice of bacon then place each one in a muffin cavity.
Bake at 375 F for 30 minutes then cook under a high broiler for 5 minutes to get the bacon crispy.
Remove from the oven and prepare.

9. CREAM CHEESE & SALAMI KETO PINWHEELS

Ingredients:
1 8oz block cream cheese
8-10 thin slices of pepperoni and genoa salami ,may need more depending on size
4 tbsp finely diced pickles

Directions:
Bring cream cheese to room temperature and whip until fluffy.
Spread cream cheese in a 1/4 inch thick rectangle in the center of a large piece of plastic wrap.
Spread pickles over cream cheese.
Place salami over cream cheese in overlapping layers so all cream cheese layer is covered.
Place a second piece of plastic wrap over salami layer and gently press down.
Flip entire rectangle over so bottom cream cheese layer is now facing the top.
Carefully peel back plastic wrap off top cream cheese layer.
Begin rolling into log shape slowly removing bottom layer of plastic wrap as you go.
Place pinwheel in tight plastic wrap and refrigerate at least 4 hours, overnight preferred.
Slice into preferred thickness.

10. CHEESEBURGER LETTUCE WRAPS

Prep time: 15 minutes
Cook time: 8 minutes
Total time: 23 minutes

Ingredients:
2 pounds lean ground beef
1/2 tsp seasoned salt
1 tsp black pepper
1 tsp dried oregano
6 slices American cheese
2 large heads iceburg or romaine lettuce, rinsed then dried
2 tomatoes, sliced thin
small red onion, sliced thin
Spread:1/4 cup light mayo
3 tbsp ketchup
1 tbsp dill pickle relish
dash of salt and pepper

Directions:
Heat a grill or skillet on medium heat.
In a large bowl, mix together ground beef, seasoned salt, pepper and oregano.
Divide mixture into 6 sections then roll each into a ball. Press each ball down flat to form a patty.

Place patties on grill/pan and cook for approximately 4 minutes on each side or until cooked to your liking. (If using a skillet, only cook 3 at a time to avoid over-crowding.)

Place a slice of cheese on each cooked burger. Place each burger on a large piece of lettuce. Top with spread , one slice tomato, red onion and whatever else you like. Wrap the lettuce up over the top and serve.

Spread: In a small bowl mix together all the spread ingredients. Refrigerate until ready to use.

11. SESAME SALMON WITH BABY BOK CHOY AND MUSHROOMS

Ingredients:
Main Dish
4 each 4-6 oz.salmon fillet
2 each portobello mushroom caps (or 8 oz. baby bella mushrooms)
4 each baby bok choy
1 tbsp toasted sesame seeds
1 each green onion
Marinade
1 tbsp olive oil
1 tsp sesame oil
1 tbsp coconut aminos
1/2 inch ginger grated (approx. 1 tsp.)
1/2 lemon juice
1/2 tsp salt
1/2 tsp black pepper

Directions:
Whisk together all of your marinade ingredients.
Drizzle half of the marinade on the salmon and turn to coat. Cover and refrigerate the salmon while it marinates for one hour.
Preheat oven to 400.

Prepare vegetables: Trim the rough ends from the bok choy and cut into halves. Slice the mushrooms into ½ inch pieces.

Drizzle the remaining marinade over the vegetables and lay on a lined baking sheet.

Place salmon, skin side down, on a lined baking sheet as well. Bake until salmon is cooked through, about 20 minutes.

Top with sliced green onions and sesame seeds.

12. BACON, CHICKEN & TOMATO STUFFED AVOCADO

Prep time: 10 minutes
Cook time: 20 minutes
Total time: 30 minutes

Ingredients:
2 chicken breasts, grilled
3 pieces bacon, cooked and chopped
2 avocado
1/3 cup grape tomatoes, chopped
1/3 cup mayo, paleo

Directions:
Sprinkle chicken with favorite seasoning, grill, and cut into cubes.
Grill bacon strips, and set aside.
Place cubed chicken in a medium bowl. Add tomatoes, onions and bacon.
Add Paleo Mayo and gently mix everything together.
Just before serving, slice avocados in half and discard pit.
Pile the chicken mix on top of each avocado half.

13. KETO CHICKEN ENCHILADA BOWL

Ingredients:

2-3 chicken breasts (about one pound of chicken)

3/4 cups red enchilada sauce

1/4 cup water

1/4 cup onion

1 4 oz can green chiles

1 12oz steam bag cauliflower rice

Preferred toppings- use avocado, jalapeno, cheese, and roma tomatoes, seasoning to taste.

Directions:

In skillet over medium heat cook chicken breasts until lightly brown.

Add enchilada sauce, chiles, onions, water and reduce heat to simmer, covered.

Cover and cook until chicken is cooked through and shred chicken.

Add chicken back into sauce and continue simmering for additional 10 minutes uncovered or until most of liquid has been soaked up.

Prepare cauliflower rice per bag instructions and dice preferred toppings.

Top rice with chicken, cheese, avocado or preferred toppings.

14. AVOCADO TUNA SALAD RECIPE

Prep time: 10 minutes

Ingredients
15 oz tuna in oil, drained and flaked (3 small cans)
1 English cucumber, sliced
2 large or 3 medium avocados peeled, pitted & sliced
1 small/medium red onion thinly sliced
1/4 cup cilantro (1/2 of a small bunch)
2 tbsp lemon juice freshly squeezed
2 tbsp extra virgin olive oil
1 tsp sea salt or to taste
1/8 tsp black pepper

Directions
In a large salad bowl, combine: sliced cucumber, sliced avocado, thinly sliced red onion, drained tuna, and 1/4 cup cilantro
Drizzle salad ingredients with 2 tbsp lemon juice, 2 tbsp olive oil, 1 tsp salt and 1/8 tsp black pepper (or season to taste). Toss to combine and serve.

15. SHEET PAN CHICKEN FAJITAS

Prep time: 15 minutes
Cook time: 20 minutes
Total time: 35 minutes

Ingredients:
1.5 lbs chicken breasts, boneless, skinless
olive oil
1 tbsp taco seasoning
3 bell peppers, sliced
1 onion, sliced thinly
fresh limes

Directions:
Preheat oven to 400ºF and grease large rimmed baking sheet.
Slice chicken into strips and season to coat with taco seasoning. Lightly drizzle seasoned chicken with olive oil.
Chop all veggies into strips. Drizzle with olive oil and more taco seasoning if desired.
Place chicken and veggies on sheet pan and bake at 400 F until chicken strips are cooked through and veggies are tender, about 20-25 minutes
Remove from oven and squeeze fresh lime over. Serve as desired in tortillas or over cauliflower rice.

16. SPICY MUSTARD THYME CHICKEN & COCONUT ROASTED BRUSSELS SPROUTS

Prep time: 10 minutes
Cook time: 25 minutes

Ingredients:
1 pound Brussels sprouts sliced in half
2 medium boneless skinless chicken breast
1/4 cup ground spicy mustard
1 tbsp lemon juice
1 tsp thyme
Salt & pepper to taste
1 tbsp coconut oil, melted

Directions:
In a small ramekin, whisk together the spicy mustard with lemon juice, salt, pepper, and thyme.
Place the two chicken breasts in a bowl and pour the mustard over them. Using a spoon, coat the chicken breasts with the mustard. Place in the refrigerator to marinate 10 minutes then remove and bring to room temperature 15 minutes prior to cooking.
Preheat oven to 350 F. Prepare a baking sheet with parchment paper.
Next, place Brussels sprouts in a medium bowl and toss with melted coconut oil, salt and pepper.

Transfer Brussels sprouts to the prepared baking sheets, spreading into an even layer.

Place marinated chicken breasts in a glass baking pan.

Place the chicken breasts in the oven baking at 350 F 10 minutes. After 10 minutes, place the Brussels sprouts in the oven.Cook both 15 minutes.

Remove from the oven and divide the meal into two servings, placing in individual meal prep containers.

17. FATHEAD PIZZA CRUST RECIPE (LOW-CARB KETO PIZZA)

Prep time: 10 minutes

Cook time: 10 minutes

Total time: 20 minutes

This low carb keto Fathead pizza crust recipe with coconut flour is so easy, with only 4 ingredients, it's the ultimate keto pizza - easy to make, chewy, and ready in 20 minutes.

Ingredients:

1 1/2 cup mozzarella cheese, shredded

2 tbsp cream cheese cut into cubes

2 large eggs, beaten

1/3 cups coconut flour

Directions:

Preheat the oven to 425° F . Line a baking sheet or pizza pan with parchment paper.

Combine the shredded mozzarella and cubed cream cheese in a large bowl. Microwave for 90 seconds, stirring halfway through. Stir again at the end until well incorporated (**see notes for an alternative to the microwave).

Stir in the beaten eggs and coconut flour. Knead with your hands until a dough forms. If the dough becomes hard before fully mixed, you can microwave for 10-15 seconds to soften it.

Spread the dough onto the lined baking pan to 1/4" or 1/3" thickness, using your hands or a rolling pin over a piece of parchment (the rolling pin works better if you have one). Use a toothpick or fork to poke lots of holes throughout the crust to prevent bubbling.

Bake for 6 minutes. Poke more holes in any places where you see bubbles forming. Bake for 3-7 more minutes, until golden brown.

Recipe notes:

To make a keto pizza, top with sauce and toppings after cooking the crust and return to the oven for about 10 minutes, until heated through.

**If you don't want to use the microwave, use a double boiler to melt the cheese and cream cheese together instead. Boil water in a saucepan, then place the cheeses in a metal bowl resting over the edges of the saucepan. The idea is to melt the cheese without burning it, stirring frequently.

Nutrition info does not include toppings.

18. KETO LASAGNA WITH ZUCCHINI NOODLES

Prep time: 15 minutes
Cook time: 30 minutes
Total time: 45 minutes

Ingredients:
16 oz ground beef
1 cup Rao's marinara sauce
1 zucchini, large
10 oz ricotta cheese
4 oz mozzarella cheese, shredded

Directions:
Preheat oven to 350° F. Peel zucchini into strips and leave out the seedy core. Salt and let sit for 15 minutes and blot with paper towels.
Brown ground beef in pan and add marinara. Season well with salt and pepper.
Layer into a small casserole dish: meat, zucchini, ricotta, meat, zucchini, ricotta, mozzarella.
Cover with foil and bake for 30 minutes. Broil uncovered for 2-3 minutes to brown the top.

19. ONE-PAN LEMON CHICKEN WITH ASPARAGUS

Prep time: 5 minutes

Cook time: 25 minutes

Total time: 30 minutes

The method here is simple enough: coat your chicken in light flour batter. You can use a regular gluten free flour or tapioca/arrowroot if you're looking for a grain free.

After you brown the chicken on both sides, you quickly braise the asparagus in the pan along with a little garlic, stock, lemon juice and mustard. Once the sauce reduces down you simply add the chicken back to the pan, sprinkle with some parsley for added freshness and you're done. All done in less than 30 minutes and in one pan.

Serve the lemon chicken & asparagus over a bed of rice/cauliflower rice to soak up all the saucy goodness. Bright and punchy lemon garlic flavours with a tangy, mustard bite .

Ingredients:

4 chicken breasts, boneless, skinless

1/4 cup tapioca flour for paleo or plain gluten-free flour

2 tbsp olive oil

3/4 tsp sea salt plus more for seasoning

1/2 tsp ground black pepper plus more for seasoning

1 pound asparagus stalks ends trimmed and then cut in half

2 cloves garlic crushed

3 tbsp fresh lemon juice

1/2 zest of lemon

1 tbsp dijon mustard

1 cup chicken stock aim for a lower sodium stock

1 tbsp fresh parsley roughly chopped, plus more for garnishing

Directions:

Place the chicken breasts between two pieces of plastic cling wrap and pound them down to make them even in thickness. This will help the chicken cook evenly and make for more tender chicken. If your breasts are extra thick you can also just cut/slice them in half.

Place the flour, salt & pepper in a shallow dish and gently toss the chicken breasts to coat in flour.

In a large skillet add one tablespoon of olive oil and bring to a medium-high heat. When the oil is hot add the chicken to the skillet and cook each side for about 5 minutes or until golden and cooked through. Once cooked remove the chicken and place on a paper towel lined plate. Set aside while you cook the asparagus.

Add the remaining 1 tablespoon olive oil in the skillet. Add the asparagus stalks and sauté for a minute. Add the garlic and sauté another minute longer until fragrant.

In a small bowl or cup whisk together the lemon juice and mustard until fully mixed.Pour into the skillet with the asparagus along with the chicken stock and the zest. Bring the liquid to a boil and then reduce down to a simmer. Cover and let cook another 3-4 minutes or until the asparagus is tender.

Stir in the parsley and then add the chicken back to the pan and rotate the breasts to coat in the liquids. Taste the sauce and season with more salt & pepper as needed.

20. CHEESY BACON-STUFFED MINI PEPPERS

Prep time: 15 minutes

Cook time: 12 minutes

Total time: 27 minutes

These Cheesy Bacon-Stuffed Mini Peppers are the perfect crowd pleasing appetizer. They're stuffed with two kinds of cheese, bacon, and more, then baked till melty and delicious!

Ingredients:

6 mini sweet peppers sliced in half, seeds and membranes removed

4 oz cream cheese

2 tbsp green onions, sliced

4 slices bacon, cooked and crumbled

1/2 tsp garlic powder

1/2 cup shredded cheddar cheese, plus extra for topping

1 tsp Worcestershire sauce

chopped cilantro for topping (optional)

Directions:

Preheat oven to 400°. Spray a cookie sheet with nonstick cooking spray and set aside.

In a small bowl, beat together the cream cheese, green onions, bacon, garlic powder, cheddar, and worcestershire sauce with an electric mixer until smooth.

Fill the sliced peppers with the filling, about a heaping tablespoon each. Place on prepared cookie sheet, then sprinkle each pepper with a little extra cheese. Bake in the preheated oven for 10-12 minutes until cheese is melted and bubbly and peppers have softened.

Allow to cool slightly before eating. Sprinkle with a little chopped cilantro if desired.

21. STEAK BITES

Prep time: 10 minuts
Cook time: 3 minuts
Marinate time: 3-24 hours

Ingredients:
1/2 cup soy sauce
1/3 cup olive oil
1/4 cup Worcestershire sauce
1 tsp minced garlic
2 tbsp dried basil
1 tbsp dried parsley
1 tsp black pepper
1-1/2 lbs flat iron or top sirloin steak, cut in 1-inch pieces

Directions:
Place all ingredients, except steak, in a large ziplock baggie. Stir with a spoon to combine.
Drop steak pieces in and seal shut. Shake gently to coat steak entirely in marinade.Place bag in refrigerator to marinate for at least 3 hours or up to 24.
Heat a large skillet over medium-high heat. Heat skillet until it's very hot. Remove steak pieces from marinade using a slotted spoon and place in hot skillet. Discard marinade. Cook steak according to your desired temperature.We like medium-well so I cooked ours for about 3 minutes.

22. KETO AVOCADO BROWNIES

Prep time: 10 minutes
Cook time: 35 minutes
Total time: 45 minutes

Ingredients:
250 g avocado about 2
1/2 tsp vanilla
4 tbsp cocoa powder
1 tsp stevia powder
3 tbsp refined coconut oil
2 eggs
100 g Lily's Dark Chocolate, melted
90 g blanched almond flour
1/4 tsp baking soda
1 tsp baking powder
1/4 tsp salt
1/4 cup erythritol

Directions:
Preheat the oven to 350F.
Peel the avocados and place in a food processor. Process until smooth.
Add each ingredient one at a time and process for a few seconds until all of the ingredients (except the dry ones) have been added to the food processor.

In a separate bowl, combine the dry ingredients together and whisk together. Add to the food processor and mix until combined.

Place a piece of parchment paper over a 30x20cm baking dish and pour the batter into it. Spoon evenly and place in the preheated oven. Bake for 35 minutes.

Take out of the oven, let cool and slice into 12 pieces.

23. COCONUT OIL FAT BOMBS

Prep time: 15 minutes
Cook time: 5 minutes
Total time: 20 minutes

These 5-ingredient coconut oil bombs melt in your mouth and pack a dose of energy!

Ingredients:
 2 cups shredded unsweetened coconut
 1/3 cup coconut oil, melted
 2 tbsp raw honey
 4 oz raw dark chocolate chips
 1/2 tsp vanilla bean powder, optional

Directions:
In a blender, add shredded coconut, coconut oil, raw honey and vanilla bean powder. Blend until mixture is fine and crumbled.
Line a small baking sheet or plate with wax paper. Using a tablespoon-size measuring spoon, scoop mixture and form into small mounds, using your hands. Set onto wax paper.Place in freezer 10 minutes to set. Using a double boiler, melt chocolate until smooth. Use a butterknife to drizzle coconut bombs with chocolate. Place back into refrigerator to set 10 minutes. Store in refrigerator.

24. KETO BREAD

Total time: 40 minutes

Ingredients:
1½ cups almond flour
6 egg whites
¼ tsp cream of tartar
3–4 tbsp butter, melted
¾ tsp baking soda
3 tsp apple cider vinegar
2 tbsp coconut flour

Directions:
Preheat oven to 375 F.
The first thing you'll need to do is separate six eggs. You'll only use the egg whites for this keto bread recipe, so feel free to set the yolks off to the side to save for another recipe. Add the cream of tartar to the egg whites and, using a hand mixer, whip the eggs until soft peaks are formed.
Add the almond flour, butter, baking soda, apple cider vinegar and coconut flour to a food processor, blending until well-incorporated.
Place the mix into a bowl and gently fold in the egg white mixture.
Grease an 8x4 loaf pan and pour in the bread mixture.

Bake for 30 minutes.

Your loaf should come out just browned on top!

Allow the bread to cool slightly before cutting into it.

Then, serve and enjoy!

25. AVOCADO DEVILED EGGS RECIPE — THE IDEAL KETO SNACK

Total time: 25 minutes

Ingredients:
4–6 eggs
1 avocado
¼ tsp sea salt
¼ tsp pepper
¼ tsp garlic
¼ tsp chili powder
¼ tsp cumin
¼ tsp smoked paprika, optional*
2 tbsp cilantro

Directions:
In a medium pot add eggs and cover with water until fully submerged.
Bring to a boil, then remove from heat and cover for 12–13 minutes.
Fill a large bowl with ice water and, using a slotted spoon, gently place eggs in the bowl, allowing eggs to chill for 5 minutes.
Remove outer casing from eggs and slice in half lengthwise, removing the yolk.
Add the yolk, along with the avocado and spices to a bowl, mixing together until well combined.

Add the mixture to the egg halves.

Drizzle with lime juice and top with cilantro.

Benefit-rich eggs are a serious powerhouse food. They're a relatively inexpensive source of meat-free protein that can help prevent disease, improve eye health and help you drop pounds. And while they're most often enjoyed as a breakfast food or a baking ingredient, they make a pretty tasty and popular appetizer in the form of deviled eggs.

26. CHOCOLATE FAT BOMBS RECIPE

Prep time: 10 minuts
Total time: 25 minuts

Ingredients:
125g/4.4 oz cream cheese
125g/4.4 oz unsalted butter
2 tbsp cacao powder
1 tbsp sweetener of choice (or more to taste)

Directions:
Place the cream cheese and butter into a large bowl and allow to soften gently at room temperature.
When softened beat briefly with an electric whisk then add the cacao powder and your sweetener of choice.
Beat until smooth.
Get out mini baking cups and place 1-2 teaspoons of the mixture into each cup.
Place into the fridge to firm and enjoy!

27. CAULIFLOWER-CRUSTED GRILLED CHEESE SANDWICHES

Ingredients:

1 medium head of cauliflower (raw), cut into small florets and stems removed

1 large egg

1/2 cup shredded Parmesan cheese

1 tsp Italian herb seasoning

2 thick slices of white cheddar cheese (you can also use shredded cheddar cheese)

Directions:

Preheat oven to 450F. Place cauliflower into food processor and pulse until crumbs about half the size of a grain of rice.

Place cauliflower into large microwave safe bowl and microwave for 2 minutes. Your cauliflower should be soft and tender (and hot!). (If you don't want to use the microwave to dry out the cauliflower and prefer to steam and wring with a cloth to dry.)

Stir cauliflower to mix up the bottom and top cauliflower. Place back into the microwave and cook for another 3 minutes. Remove and stir again so that all the cauliflower cooks evenly. Place back into microwave and cook for 5 minutes. At this point, you should see the cauliflower is starting to become more dry. Microwave for another 5 minutes. Cauliflower should still be slightly moist to the touch, but should look dry and clumped up, If you've made cauliflower pizza or breadsticks with the cloth wringing dry method,

Allow cauliflower to cool for a few minutes. Then add in egg and cheese. Stir to combine until smooth paste forms. Stir in seasoning. Divide dough into 4 equal parts. Place onto large baking sheet lined with parchment paper.Using your knuckles and fingers, shape into square bread slices about 1/3 inch thick.Bake cauliflower bread for about 15-18 minutes or until golden brown. Remove from oven and let cool a few minutes.

Using a good spatula, carefully slide cauliflower bread off of parchment paper. Now you are ready to assemble your sandwiches. You can do this a few different ways. You can either cook on the stove top as you would normally cook a grilled cheese. You can also place sandwiches into toaster oven and broil for several minutes (5-10) until cheese is completely melted and bread is toasty. If you don't own a toaster oven, you can also do this in the oven.

28. CHICKEN PAD THAI

Prep time: 20 minutes
Cook time: 10 minutes
Total time: 30 minutes

This chicken pad thai recipe is extremely healthy and nutritious meal, it can be prepared ahead of time.

Ingredients:
⅛ tsp ground ginger
⅛ tsp garlic powder
⅛ tsp sea salt
⅛ tsp freshly ground black pepper
2 pounds free-range chicken tenders
2 tbsp peanut oil
3 large free-range eggs, lightly beaten
⅓ cup organic chicken broth
3 tbsp peanut butter
2 tbsp tamari
1 tbsp rice vinegar
½ cup chopped scallion
2 garlic cloves, minced
1 tsp red pepper flakes
4 zucchini, spiralized
½ cup bean sprouts
½ cup crushed peanuts, for garnish
1 lime, cut into wedges, for garnish

Directions:

In a medium bowl, mix the ginger, garlic powder, salt, and black pepper. Add the chicken tenders and toss until coated.

In a medium skillet, heat the peanut oil over medium-high heat. When the oil is hot, add the chicken tenders and cook, turning once, until cooked through, about 3 minutes. Remove the chicken from the skillet and cut into ¼-inch-thick slices.Set aside.

Add the eggs to the skillet and scramble them for about 1 minute. Remove the scrambled eggs from the skillet and set aside.

Reduce the heat under the skillet to medium-low and add the chicken broth, peanut butter, tamari, vinegar, scallion, garlic, and red pepper flakes. Stir well and cook for 3 minutes.

Add the chicken slices, zucchini noodles, scrambled eggs, and sprouts to the skillet. Toss to coat with the sauce, and cook for about 1 minute.

Serve the pad thai garnished with the peanuts and lime wedges.

29. CINNAMON BUTTER FAT BOMBS

Ingredients:

1 lb salted butter, preferably grass-fed

1/4 cup honey (OR, substitute all or part of the honey with your favorite low-calorie sweetener to taste; personally I like 1 tablespoon honey and 20 drops SweetLeaf clear liquid stevia)

1 tbsp cinnamon

1 1/2 tsp vanilla extract

Salt to taste, if using unsalted butter

Directions:

Allow butter to soften on your counter until it is slightly squishy.

Add butter, cinnamon, honey/stevia, and vanilla extract to your food processor. Process for a couple of minutes to mix ingredients and achieve slightly whipped taste. Stop food processor as necessary to scrape down the bowl and reincorporate ingredients.

Spoon butter mixture into silicone molds, Alternatively, you can line a cutting board or other flat surface with parchment paper and then spoon dollops of butter mixture onto the parchment paper.

Freeze for an hour or two, then remove from parchment paper or molds and store in a container in your freeze.

30. COCONUT OIL MAYONNAISE

Total time: 10 minutes

Ingredients:

2 egg yolks at room temperature

1 tsp mustard

2 tsp fresh lemon juice

½ cup olive oil

¾ cup of coconut oil, melted

pinch of sea salt and black pepper

Directions:

In a blender, add egg yolks, mustard, 1 teaspoon fresh lemon juice and blend on very low setting.

Slowly drizzle in the oil while blender is still on low speed.

Once oil is well incorporated, add the remaining lemon juice.

Add salt and pepper, to taste.

Place mayo in a jar and store in the refrigerator.

31. CREAMY CAULIFLOWER MASH AND KETO GRAVY

Total time: 1 hour

Ingredients:
5 cups cauliflower chopped
4 tbsp heavy whipping cream
3 tbsp Butter
5 cloves garlic minced
2 tsp dried rosemary
3 tbsp parmesan
1/2 tsp pepper
Pink salt (to taste)

Directions:
Chop up 5 cups of raw cauliflower.
Bring pot of water to a boil (enough to cover all the cauliflower), add the cauliflower and boil for 15 minutes or until tender.
Drain cauliflower and place in processor.
Cook butter, garlic and rosemary in a saucepan over medium heat until fragrant.
Add melted butter, garlic and rosemary to processor and pulse several times until well combined.
Add cream, parmesan, salt and pepper to processor and process until smooth and creamy.
Taste for salt level. Serve warm.

32. CRUSTLESS SPINACH QUICHE RECIPE

Total time: 40 minutes

Ingredients:
1 tbsp coconut oil
1 onion, chopped
1 package frozen chopped spinach, thawed and drained
8 eggs, beaten
3 cups shredded raw cheese
¼ tsp sea salt
⅛ tsp black pepper

Directions:
Preheat oven to 350° F and grease a 9 inch pie pan with coconut oil.
Heat coconut oil, and onions over medium heat in sauce pan until onions are soft. Stir in spinach and cook until excess moisture has evaporated.
In a bowl, combine eggs, cheese, salt and pepper. Add spinach mixture and blend.
Scoop into pan and bake for 30 minutes.

33. SIMPLE PALEO CHICKEN CURRY RECIPE

Prep time: 30 minutes

Cook time: 30 minutes

Ingredients:

2 tbsp coconut oil (or oil of your choice)

8 chicken thighs, boneless skinless, cut into 1" pieces

1 large onion, cut into large chunks

3 small zucchini, cut half lengthwise and thickly sliced

1 tsp garlic, minced

1 tbsp curry powder

1/2 tsp paprika

2 tsp salt

2 cans coconut milk (about 15 oz each)

1 cup tomatoes

cilantro (to garnish)

Directions:

Heat the olive oil in a stock pot to high heat. Add the chicken and cook until chicken pieces are browned on both sides. Remove the chicken from the pan and set aside, keeping the remaining oil in the stock pot.

Add the onion and zucchini and saute until lightly browned. Add the garlic, curry powder, paprika, and salt and saute for 30 seconds.

Add the chicken back into the pot, along with the coconut milk. Bring to a boil.

Reduce heat to a simmer, cover the pot with a lid, and let simmer for 30 minutes, or until chicken is tender. Add the tomatoes to the pot in the last 5 minutes of cooking.

Serve in a bowl with the coconut broth, like a soup.Top with cilantro.

34. CAULIFLOWER MAC AND CHEESE

Total time: 30-40 minutes

Ingredients:
1 large cauliflower head, cut into small florets
½-¾ cup kefir
½ cup goat's milk cottage cheese, pureed
1½ tsp Dijon mustard
1½ cups grated sheep's or goat's milk cheddar cheese, plus additional for topping
½ tsp black pepper
1 tsp sea salt
⅛ tsp garlic powder

Directions:
Preheat oven to 375° F. Grease 8" x 8" pan with ghee. Bring a pot of salted water to a boil. Add cauliflower and cook until slightly tender, about 5 minutes. Drain and pat dry with paper towels. Spread in prepared pan.
In a saucepan over medium-high heat, mix together kefir, cottage cheese, and mustard until smooth.
In a saucepan over medium high heat, mix together the cottage cheese, kefir and mustard until smooth
Stir in cheese, sea salt, black pepper, and garlic powder until cheese just starts to melt. Pour over cauliflower and stir. Top with additional cheese if desired and bake for 10–15 minutes.

35. JALAPENO CHEDDAR BURGERS
(TURKEY OR BEEF)

Prep time: 15 minutes
Cook time: 15 minutes
Total time: 30 minutes

Ingredients:
28 oz lean turkey or beef (not extra lean)
2 tbsp finely minced onion
salt & pepper to taste
4 tbsp cream cheese
2 oz shredded cheddar cheese
1/4 tsp garlic powder
1 fresh jalapeno pepper, diced (seeds removed if you prefer less spice)
1 tbsp olive oil
Rolls & Toppings as desired

Directions:
Preheat grill to medium or oven to broil on high.
In a small bowl combine cream cheese, cheddar cheese, garlic powder and diced jalapeno.
Combine meat, salt & pepper and minced onion. Divide meat into 4 even pieces (7oz each). Take 1/4 of the cream cheese mixture and flatten it into a pancake shape. Wrap beef or turkey around the cheese ensuring the cheese mixture is completely

covered. Brush each burger with a little bit of olive oil.

To Grill:

Grill burgers over medium heat for 6-7 minutes on each side or until completely cooked. (Turkey should reach an internal temperature of 165 degrees and beef should reach 160° F.)

To Broil:

Place burgers on a foil covered pan approximately 6" from the broiler. Broil 5-6 minutes on each side or until completely cooked. (Turkey should reach an internal temperature of 165° and beef should reach 160° F.)

36. ONION SOUP

Total time: 45–60 minutes

Ingredients:
4 large onions, peeled and thinly sliced
2 cups chicken bone broth
2 cups beef bone broth
4 tbsp ghee
5 garlic cloves, chopped
Goat cheese, for topping (optional)
Sea salt and black pepper to taste

Directions:
In a stock pot over medium heat, melt ghee and thinly sliced onions.
Cook onions until lightly caramelized.
Add bone broth and garlic.
Season with salt and pepper to taste.
Bring mixture to a boil and then reduce the heat and allow to simmer for 30–50 minutes (the longer, the more flavor).
Soup, glorious soup. It's such an easy way to start a multi-course meal or, paired with a side salad and sprouted bread, a simple lunch or dinner. And there's no better — or easier — soup than this onion soup recipe. You've likely had French onion when out, or maybe even from a can, but no more. With this easy onion soup recipe, you can enjoy homemade, healthy onion soup whenever the mood strikes.

37. BABA GANOUSH

Prep time: 20 minutes
Total time: 30 minutes

Ingredients:
1 eggplant, sliced
1 cup tahini
3–4 garlic cloves, smashed
1–2 tbsp avocado oil
1 cup parsley, chopped
Sea salt and pepper to taste

Directions:
On a baking sheet lined with parchment paper, lay out the eggplant slices.
Salt the eggplant and allow eggplant to sit for 15–20 minutes to remove moisture.
Use a paper towel to dab eggplant, removing excess water.
Broil eggplant on top oven rack for 5–8 minutes.
Remove skin (optional).
Place eggplant in a food processor and pulse until broken down.
Place all other ingredients in the food processor and blend on high until well combined.
Serve with chopped vegetables.

38. PIZZA GRILLED CHICKEN

Prep time: 15 minutes

Cook time: 15 minutes

Total time: 25 minutes

Ingredients:

1 boneless skinless chicken breast

1/2 tbsp olive oil

1 clove garlic, minced

1/2 cup half & half or heavy whipping cream

1/4 tsp xanthan gum thickener

1 cup fresh spinach, roughly chopped

1/2 cup part-skim shredded mozzarella

Sea salt & pepper to taste

Fathead Dough:

2oz cream cheese

3/4 cup shredded mozzarella

1 egg, beaten

1/4 tsp garlic powder

1/3 cup almond flour

Directions:

To make the pizza crust,

Melt mozzarella and cream cheese in the microwave for 30 seconds at a time. Mixing often.

In a separate bowl mix beaten egg with almond flour and remaining dough ingredients.

Combine cheese mixture with flour and mix. Mix. Keep mixing! Once a sticky dough consistency has been reached, refrigerate while preparing sauce and chicken.

Saute the chicken in a skillet over medium heat until done.Remove, set aside.

Add garlic plus the xantham gum with half & half to the skillet and bring to a boil. Reduce to simmer when sauce starts to thicken.

Fold in spinach, cook just until wilted.

Using hands, work dough out into a circle on a pizza pan. Bake on 350 for 10 minutes. Crust must be pre-baked to hold up to the sauce and toppings.

Spread sauce/spinach mixture onto your cooked pizza crust. Top with chicken and shredded cheese

Bake 5 minutes or until cheese is melted.

NOTE* if your oven and pizza crust weren't already hot from making the dough, bake for 10 minutes instead.

39. BURGER COOK MUSHROOOM

Ingredients:

1 pound grass fed beef

24 baby portabella mushrooms

4 slices sharp cheddar, sliced into quarters

4 tbsp chopped yellow onion

2 dill pickles, sliced

2 tbsp extra virgin olive oil

12 basil leaves

yellow mustard, mayo, sriracha or low carb ketchup (optional)

salt and pepper to taste

Directions:

Remove stems from portabella mushroom caps and wipe with a damp paper towel to remove any dirt or debris. In a small saucepan, heat 1 tablespoon olive oil over medium heat. Add mushroom caps and cook for 2 minutes on each side, allowing mushrooms to cook through but retain firmness.

Remove mushrooms from pan and place on paper towels to allow liquid to drain off.

Divide the ground beef into 12 portions, rolling each into a small disc shape. Add salt and pepper to taste. In a large grill pan, heat remaining tbsp olive oil over medium heat. Once the pan is hot, add the meat and allow to cook for 3 minutes on one side. Flip and allow to cook for 3 minutes on the other side. Cook to desired level of doneness.

Stack a mushroom, burger, cheese, onion, pickles and your choice of condiments. Top with second mushroom cap and add a basil leaf for garnish. Use a toothpick to hold.

40. EASY CHOCOLATE MOUSSE

Ingredients:

8 oz cream cheese block, softened

¼ cup unsweetened cocoa powder

½ large avocado, pitted

⅛ tsp vanilla extract

2-3 tbsp of desired sweetener, I recommend Swerve.

¼ cup heavy whipping cream

90% dark chocolate, shaved for garnish

Directions:

Beat together the cream cheese until creamy and smooth using a handheld mixer in a medium mixing bowl. Slowly mix in the cocoa powder. Beat in the avocado and mix until creamy smooth, approximately 5 minutes.

Add the vanilla extract and sweetener and beat again until smooth, approximately 1-2 minutes.

In a separate mixing bowl, whip the heavy cream until stiff peaks form.

Place the whipped cream in the chocolate mixture and gently fold until it's incorporated.

Place the chocolate mousse in a piping bag and pipe into desired containers. Garnish with dark chocolate shavings.

41. LOW-CARB TACOS

Prep time: 30 minutes
Cook time: 30 minutes
Total time: 1 hour

Ingredients:
Cheese Taco Shells:
2 cups cheddar cheese, shredded

Taco Meat:
1 lb ground beef
1 tbsp chili powder
2 tsp cumin
1 tsp onion powder
1/2 tsp garlic powder
1/4 tsp salt
1/4 cup water
Toppings for taco: Sour cream, avocado, cheese, lettuce, etc.

Directions:
Preheat oven to 350F.

On a baking sheet lined with parchment paper or a silicone mat place 1/4 cup piles of cheese 2 inches apart. Press the cheese down lightly so it makes one layer.

Place baking sheet in the oven and bake for 5-7 minutes or until the edges of the cheese are brown.

Let the cheese cool for 2-3 minutes then lift it up and place it over the handle of a spoon or other utensil that is balanced on two cups.

Let cheese cool completely then remove.

While you continue to bake your cheese taco shells place the ground beef in a skillet over medium high heat cooking until it is completely cooked through.

Drain the grease from the meat and then add the cumin, chili powder, onion, powder, garlic powder, and salt. Pour water into skillet and stir everything around mixing it together.

Simmer for 5 minutes or until liquid has cooked away.

Add meat to taco shells and top with your favorite taco toppings.

42. ALFREDO RECIPE

Total time: 15 minutes

Ingredients:
1 small head of cauliflower, chopped (about 3 heaping cups)
2 tbsp olive oil
2 cloves garlic, smashed and minced
2 tsp pine nuts
2¼ cup almond milk
2 tsp of each: salt, pepper, oregano, and basil
juice of half a lemon
¼ cup plus 1 tbsp nutritional yeast

Directions:
In a medium-sized pot, cook the olive oil, garlic and pine nuts over medium heat for 3–4 minutes, or until garlic is golden brown.
Add in the almond milk and bring to a boil.
Reduce heat to medium and add the cauliflower and spices and cook until cauliflower is soft (about 8 minutes).
Transfer to a high-powered blender and add in the lemon juice and nutritional yeast and blend on high until smooth.
Add over your favorite gluten-free pasta or zoodles and top with fresh basil.

43. LOW-CARB BLUEBERRY MUFFINS

Ingredients:
½ stick (2 oz) butter, very soft
4 tbsp (2 oz) cream cheese, very soft
1/2 tsp vanilla
½ cup coconut flour
¼ cup Swerve Granulated
1 tsp baking powder
1/4 tsp salt
1/16 tsp cinnamon
1/8 tsp xanthan gum
3 large eggs
1/4 cup heavy cream
1/3 cup fresh blueberries
2 tsp Swerve Granulated

Directions:
Preheat oven to 350°. Position oven rack to the lower third of the oven. Line a 6-cup muffin tin with paper liners. Add the dry ingredients together in a smaller bowl and whisk together to combine and break up any lumps.

In a medium bowl, cream the butter, cream cheese, and vanilla together until light and fluffy. Add 1 egg and beat into the butter mixture until the mixture is light and fluffy (it may break or separate, it's okay). Add 1/3 of the dry ingredients and mix until completely incorporated, making sure to keep that light, fluffy texture. Keep in mind that we want a light and fluffy – almost mousse-like texture throughout this process.

Add another egg and beat until fully combined and the batter is fluffy. Add half of the remaining dry ingredients, beating again. Add the last egg, beating until fully incorporated, followed by the last of the dry ingredients. Finish by adding the heavy cream, once again, beating until the batter is thick, but still light and fluffy.Fold in the blueberries.

Spoon the thick batter into a plastic zip-loc bag and snip off a corner, producing about a 3/4 inch hole. Place the snipped corner into a muffin liner and squeeze the batter into a fat, rounded mound, filling the muffin liner about 3/4 full. Repeat for each muffin liner, adding any remaining batter to those that need a little more. Knock down any peaks with your finger. Sprinkle about ¼ teaspoon of Swerve granulated over the top of each muffin to help prevent burning and to give the muffins a nice look.

Place the muffins into the oven. Turn the oven up to 400° degrees for 5 minutes. Then, turn the oven back to 350° and bake the blueberry muffins for about 25 minutes more. They're ready when they feel firm when lightly pressed with a finger, but still sound a little moist. Remove from the oven and let cool five minutes before gently removing from the pan and placing on a cooling rack.

44. KETO BEEF WITH BROCCOLI

Prep time: 15 minutes
Cook time: 10 minutes
Total time: 25 minutes

Ingredients:
1 lb beef (sirloin, skirt steak, boneless short ribs...etc.)
1 to 2 heads broccoli, break into florets
2 cloves garlic, minced
2 pieces thin sliced ginger, finely chopped
Ghee or cooking fat of your choice

Beef marinade:
2 tbsp coconut aminos
1/2 tsp coarse sea salt
1 tbsp sesame oil
1/4 tsp black pepper
1 tsp arrowroot/sweet potato powder
1/4 tsp baking soda Baking soda is whole 30 friendly.
See notes section.

Sauce combo:
2 tbsp coconut aminos
1 tbsp red boat fish sauce
2 tsp sesame oil
1/4 tsp black pepper

Directions:

Slice beef into about ¼ inch thin. Marinate thin sliced beef with ingredients under "beef marinade". Mix well. Place broccoli florets in a microwave safe container. Add 1-2 tablespoons water. Loosely covered with a lid or wet paper towel and microwave for 2 minutes. Cook until broccoli is tender but still crunchy. Set aside.

Heat a wok over medium heat with 1 ½ tablespoons ghee. When hot, lower the heat to medium, add garlic and ginger.Season with a small pinch of salt and stir-fry until fragrant (about 10 seconds).

Turn up the heat to medium-high, add marinated beef. Spread beef evenly over the bottom of the saute pan and cook until the edge of the beef is slightly darkened and crispy. Do the same thing for flip slide - about ¾ way cooked through with slightly charred and crispy surface.

Add "Sauce Combo". Stir-fry about 1 minute. Add broccoli. Stir-fry another 30 seconds. Toss everything to combine.

45. EASY CROCKPOT CHICKEN STEW

Prep time: 5 minutes
Cook time: 2 hours
Total time: 2 hours 5 minutes

Ingredients:
2 cups chicken stock
2 medium carrots (1/2 cup), peeled and finely diced
2 celery sticks (1 cup), diced
½ onion (1/2 cup), diced
28 oz skinless and deboned chicken thighs diced into 1" pieces
1 spring fresh rosemary or ½ tsp dried rosemary
3 garlic cloves, minced
¼ tsp dried thyme
½ tsp dried oregano
1 cup fresh spinach
½ cup heavy cream
salt and pepper, to taste
xantham gum, to desired thickness, starting at ⅛ tsp
Directions:
Place the chicken stock, carrots, celery, onion, chicken thighs, rosemary, garlic, thyme, and oregano into a 3-quart crockpot or larger. Cook on high for 2 hours or on low for 4 hours.
Add salt and pepper, to taste.
Stir in spinach and heavy cream.

Sprinkle and thicken with xantham gum to desired thickness starting at ⅛th teaspoon. Continue to whisk until mix and cook for another 10 minutes.

46. KETO OATMEAL

Prep time: 2 minutes

Total time: 12 hours 2 minutes

You can substitute heavy whipping cream, coconut milk, and almond into any recipe. Generally you will need 75% as much almond milk as you need coconut milk or heavy cream. It's recommended to use chia seeds whenever almond milk is used to create a thicker consistency.

Ingredients:

Pumpkin Pie:

3 tbsp hemp hearts

1 tbsp 100% pumpkin puree

1/2 tsp pumpkin pie spice

1 tsp chia aeeds

2 drops liquid Stevia

3 tbsp unsweetened almond milk

Almond Joy:

3 tbsp hemp hearts

1/2 tbsp chopped almonds

1/2 tbsp Lily's Chocolate Chips

1/2 tbsp unsweetened shredded coconut

1/4 cup coconut milk

1 drop liquid Stevia

Double Chocolate:

3 tbsp hemp hearts

1 tbsp unsweetened cocoa powder

1/2 tbsp Lily's Chocolate Chips

1/4 tsp pink salt

1/4 cup heavy whipping cream

1 tsp chia seeds

2 drops liquid Stevia

Maple Walnut:

3 tbsp hemp hearts

1 tbsp walnuts, chopped

1/2 tbsp sugar-free maple syrup

1/2 tsp ground cinnamon

3 tbsp unsweetened almond milk

1 tsp chia seeds

Peanut Butter:

3 tbsp hemp hearts

1 tbsp peanut butter

1 tsp chia seeds

1 drop liquid Stevia

3 tbsp unsweetened almond milk

Broats:

3 tbsp hemp hearts

1 tbsp protein powder

1 tsp chia seeds
1/4 cup heavy whipping cream

Turmeric-Vanilla:
3 tbsp hemp hearts
1/4 cup coconut milk
1 tsp chia seeds
1/2 tsp turmeric powder
1/2 tsp vanilla extract
2 drops liquid Stevia

Directions:
Add all ingredients to a bowl or mason jar. Mix together thoroughly.
Place in the refrigerator overnight, or a minimum of 4 hours. Open the next day and enjoy!

47. LEMON THYME CHICKEN

Ingredients:
2 lb grass-fed beef or pork
1 1/2 tsp sea salt
1 tsp ground black pepper
2 large pastured eggs
1 medium onion, peeled and finely chopped
2 cups mushrooms (any kind will do), finely chopped
1/2 cup finely chopped OR grated carrots
2 loosely-packed cups of spinach, finely chopped
1 tsp dry thyme
3 cloves of garlic, peeled and minced
1 1/2 tbsp Dijon mustard

Directions:
Preheat your oven to 350 degrees F.
In a large bowl combine all of the ingredients. Using freshly washed hands, mix the ingredients until everything is blended together evenly.
Portion out the meat mixture evenly between a 12-hole muffin tin.
Bake for 25-30 minutes or until meat is cooked.
Enjoy warm with cauliflower rice, a salad, or side of choice.
Freeze leftovers or store in fridge for up to 5 days.

48. KETO PANCAKES

Total time: 20 minutes

Ingredients:
½ cup plus 1 tbsp almond flour
½ cup grass-fed cream cheese
4 eggs
½ tsp cinnamon
1 tbsp butter or avocado oil, for frying

Directions:
Mix all ingredients in a blender.
In a frying pan, over medium heat, add in the butter or oil.
Pour in 2–3 tablespoons of batter per pancake and turn over once the center begins to bubble (usually takes about 3–4 minutes).
Top with butter and cinnamon

49. KETO CHOCOLATE CHIA PUDDING

Ingredients:
 1 (13.5 oz) can full-fat coconut milk, blended
1 cup water
2 tbsp cacao powder
⅛ tsp vanilla stevia
⅛ tsp Celtic sea salt
¼ cup chia seeds

Directions:
In a vitamix, combine coconut milk, water, cacao powder, stevia, and salt.
Blend until smooth.
Transfer mixture to a one quart mason jar.
Add chia seeds and shake well.
Refrigerate overnight to let chia seeds soften and absorb liquid.
Notes: For this recipe, it's important to blend the coconut milk in a high-powered blender. This way you'll have a smooth and creamy pudding, rather than one with little lumps of coconut milk in it.

50. CHEESY GARLIC CREAMED SPINACH

Total time: 5 - 10 minutes

Ingredients:
3 tbsp butter
4 cloves garlic, minced
2 lb fresh spinach leaves
sea salt and black pepper, to taste
1 cup heavy cream
1/4 cup grated Parmesan cheese
1/4 cup shredded mozzarella cheese
1/4 cup goat cheese

Directions:
In a large sauté pan over medium heat, melt the butter. Add the garlic and sauté for 1 minute, being careful not to burn it.
Add the spinach. Season with sea salt and black pepper to taste.Sauté until the spinach is wilted. Remove the spinach from the pan and let it drain. You may need to press it in a colander to remove all of the excess moisture.
To the same pan, add the heavy cream, Parmesan, mozzarella and goat cheeses. Lower the heat to low and allow the sauce to thicken, 5 to 10 minutes. Add the wilted spinach back to the pan and toss until evenly coated in the creamy cheese sauce.

51. CHICKEN IN WHITE SAUCE

Prep time: 10 minutes
Cook time: 40 minutes
Total time: 50 minutes

Ingredients:
4 chicken breasts, medium sized
1 cup coconut cream
1 cup white wine
300 g mushrooms
300 g green beans, halved
2 tsp Dijon mustard
4 cloves garlic
¼ cup olive oil
1 tsp fresh thyme, chopped
1 tsp salt
1 tsp pepper

Directions:
Preheat the oven to 355F (180C).
Heat a frying pan to medium heat with half the amount of olive oil required for the recipe, add the chicken breasts and cook each side for 2 minutes.
Place the chicken on baking tray lined with baking paper. Cook for 15 minutes.

Meanwhile, in the same frying pan, slice the mushrooms and slightly brown them using the reaining olive oil and garlic.

Add the beans, coconut cream, white wine, dijon mustard, thyme, salt and pepper. Mix around in the pan and reduce to a simmer. The sauce should be quite watery to start with, and will reduce to a lovely creamy sauce.

Once the chicken has reached 15 minutes, remove from the oven. Plate the chicken and cover with sauce, mushrooms, and beans.

52. GUILTLESS GARLIC PARMESAN WINGS

Total time: 35 minutes

Ingredients:
12 chicken wings
1½ tbsp avocado oil
1 tbsp garlic powder
½ cup parmesan, grated
½ cup pecorino romano, grated
1 tsp salt
1 tsp pepper

Directions:
Preheat oven to 350 F.
Line a baking sheet with parchment and set aside.
Mix spices and cheeses in a bowl.
Coat the wings in oil.
Dip wings in mixture.
Bake for 30 minutes.

53. EGGPLANT ROLLATINI RECIPE

Total time: 1 hour

Ingredients:
2 large eggplants, sliced lengthwise
½ tsp sea salt
½ tsp black pepper
1–1½ cups marinara sauce
2 large eggs
3 cups spinach
1 package goat feta (4 oz)
1 tsp dried oregano
1 tsp parsley
1 tsp dried basil
2 cups pecorino romano, grated
1 cup raw sheep cheese, grated

Directions:
Preheat oven to 450 F.
While your oven is heating up, cut the ends off of the two eggplants and then slice lengthwise.
Place the eggplant slices on a baking sheet lined with parchment paper and sprinkle with salt and pepper.
Bake for 12–15 minutes, remove and allow to cool.
Reduce heat to 400 F.
In a medium bowl, mix the eggs, goat cheese, spinach, oregano, parsley, basil, 1 cup pecorino

romano, ½ cup raw sheep cheese, salt and pepper, mixing until well combined.

In a 9x13 baking dish, add ¾ cup marinara.

Place ¼ cup cheese mixture onto one end of the sliced eggplant, then roll it up and transfer to baking dish, continuing until baking dish is full.

Cover with remaining marinara and cheese.

Bake for 25 minutes and allow to cool for 10 minutes before serving.

54. KETO SMOOTHIE RECIPE WITH AVOCADO, CHIA SEEDS & CACAO

Total time: 15 minutes

Ingredients:
1–1¼ cups full-fat coconut milk
½ frozen avocado
1 tbsp nut butter of choice
1 tbsp chia seeds, soaked in 3 tablespoons of water for 10 minutes
2 tsp cacao nibs, cacao powder or cocoa powder or 1 scoop of chocolate protein powder made from bone broth
1 tbsp coconut oil
ice (optional)

For topping:
cacao nibs and cinnamon
¼ cup water, if needed

Directions:
Add ingredients into a high-powered blender, processing until well-combined.
Top with cacao nibs and cinnamon.

55. LOW-CARB CAULIFLOWER POT PIES

Prep time: 15 minutes
Cook time: 25 minutes
Total time: 40 minutes

Ingredients:
Cauliflower Base:
1 medium head cauliflower (4-5 cups cauliflower rice)
1/4 cup shredded parmesan cheese
1 egg
pinch of salt and pepper

Pot Pie Filling:
1/2 onion, diced
1 1/2 cups chicken broth
1/4 cup almond milk, unsweetened
1 cup frozen mixed vegetables
8 oz cooked chicken, diced
1 tbsp onion powder
1/2 tsp salt
1/2 tsp black pepper
2 tbs cornstarch, plus 1/4 cup water

Instructions:
Preheat oven to 400° F. Add the cauliflower to the bowl of a food processor and pulse until you achieve a rice-like consistency. Transfer cauliflower "rice" to a

bowl and microwave for 5 minutes. Set aside and allow cauliflower to cool for approx 10 minutes.

Add the cauliflower rice to a cheesecloth and squeeze out as much of the juice from the cauliflower as possible. If you don't, the bases may end up soggy (the key here is to really get as much of that juice out as you can). Once you have done a round with the cheesecloth. Repeat with another dry cheesecloth to ensure you have removed a majority of the liquid.

Add the dried cauliflower rice to a bowl with the egg, parmesan cheese, salt and pepper. Using your hands, combine all of the ingredients thoroughly. Spray a large muffin pan or 4 ramekins and gently press the cauliflower mixture to the sides, creating a cauliflower bowl. Bake for 20-25 minutes or until the centers are dry and the edges are golden brown.

While the cauliflower bases are in the oven, spray a medium saucepan with cooking spray and saute the diced onion on high heat until slightly tender. Reduce heat to medium and add the chicken broth, almond milk, mixed vegetables, onion powder, salt and black pepper. Stir and cover for approx 5-8 minutes or until frozen vegetables are soft.

Mix the cornstarch with the water to make a slurry and add to the sauce with the cooked chicken. Stir in the cornstarch mixture and increase heat to high and cook until sauce begins to boil. Remove from heat.

Fill each cauliflower base with the pot pie filling and serve.

56. JALAPENO POPPERS

Total time: 25 minutes

Ingredients:
10–12 jalapeno peppers, stemmed removed, sliced in
½ length-wise and seeds removed
1 package turkey bacon (optional*)
½-1 cup goat feta
½-1 cup shredded goat cheese
½ tsp cumin
½ tsp chili powder
½ tsp smoked paprika
½ tsp oregano
salt and pepper to taste

Directions:
Preheat oven to 350 F.
Line a baking sheet, or two, with parchment paper and set aside.
In a medium-sized bowl add everything except the jalapeños and turkey bacon, mixing until well-combined.
Using your hands, fill each halved jalapeño with the cheese mixture.
Wrap jalapeno with turkey bacon and place on baking sheet.
Bake for 20 minutes.
Pair with our Avocado Ranch Dressing.

57. KETO LOW-CARB GRANOLA CEREAL

Prep time: 10 minutes
Cook time: 15 minutes
Total time: 25 minutes

Ingredients:
1 cup almonds
1 cup hazelnuts
1 cup pecans
1/3 cup pumpkin seeds
1/3 cup sunflower seeds
6 tbsp Erythritol
1/2 cup golden flaxseed meal
1 large egg white
1/4 cup butter (measured solid, then melted; can use coconut oil or ghee for dairy-free)
1 tsp vanilla extract

Directions:
Preheat oven to 325° F. Line a large baking sheet, or two small ones, with parchment paper.
Pulse almonds and hazelnuts in a food processor intermittently, until most of the nuts are in chopped into large pieces (about 1/4 to 1/2 of the full size of the nuts).

Add the pecans. Pulse again, stopping when the pecans are in large pieces (pecans are added later since they are softer).

Add the pumpkin seeds, sunflower seeds, erythritol, and golden flaxseed meal. Pulse just until everything is mixed well. Don't over-process! You want to have plenty of nut pieces remaining, and most of the seeds should be intact.

Add the egg white to the food processor. Whisk together the melted butter and vanilla extract in a small bowl, and evenly pour that in, too.

Pulse a couple times, mix a little from the bottom toward the top with a spatula, then pulse a couple times again. Repeat as needed until everything is coated evenly. Again, avoid over-processing. At the end of this step, you'll have a combination of coarse meal and nut pieces, and everything should be a little damp from the egg white and butter.

Transfer the nut mixture to the prepared baking sheet in a uniform layer, pressing together into a thin rectangle (about 1/4 to 1/3 in (.6-.8 cm) thick). Bake for 15-18 minutes, until lightly browned, especially at the edges.

Cool completely before breaking apart into pieces (the granola will be soft when you remove it from the oven, but will crisp up as it cools).

58. KETO ZUCCHINI BREAD WITH WALNUTS

Ingredients:
3 large eggs
½ cup olive oil
1 tsp vanilla extract
2 ½ cups almond flour
1 ½ cups erythritol
½ tsp salt
1 ½ tsp baking powder
½ tsp nutmeg
1 tsp ground cinnamon
¼ tsp ground ginger
1 cup grated zucchini
½ cup chopped walnuts

Directions:
Preheat oven to 350°F. Whisk together the eggs, oil, and vanilla extract. Set to the side.
In another bowl, mix together the almond flour, erythritol, salt, baking powder, nutmeg, cinnamon, and ginger. Set to the side.
Using a cheesecloth or paper towel, take the zucchini and squeeze out the excess water.
Then, whisk the zucchini into the bowl with the eggs.
Slowly add the dry ingredients into the egg mixture using a hand mixer until fully blended.

Lightly spray a 9×5 loaf pan, and spoon in the zucchini bread mixture.

Then, spoon in the chopped walnuts on top of the zucchini bread. Press walnuts into the batter using a spatula.

Bake for 60-70 minutes at 350°F or until the walnuts on top look browned.

59. KETO WALNUT BREAD

Ingredients:
3 large eggs
½ cup olive oil
1 tsp vanilla extract
2 1/2 cups almond flour
1 1/2 cups erythritol
½ tsp salt
1 1/2 tsp baking powder
½ tsp nutmeg
1 tsp ground cinnamon
¼ tsp ground ginger
1 cup grated zucchini
½ cup chopped walnuts

Directions:
Preheat oven to 350°F. Whisk together the eggs, oil, and vanilla extract. Set to the side.
In another bowl, mix together the almond flour, erythritol, salt, baking powder, nutmeg, cinnamon, and ginger. Set to the side.
Using a cheesecloth or paper towel, take the zucchini and squeeze out the excess water.
Then, whisk the zucchini into the bowl with the eggs.
Slowly add the dry ingredients into the egg mixture using a hand mixer until fully blended.

Lightly spray a 9x5 loaf pan, and spoon in the zucchini bread mixture.

Then, spoon in the chopped walnuts on top of the zucchini bread. Press walnuts into the batter using a spatula.

Bake for 60-70 minutes at 350°F or until the walnuts on top look browned.

60. LOW-CARB TORTILLA CHIPS

Prep time: 10 minutes
Cook time: 10 minutes
Total time: 20 minutes

Ingredients:
2 cups almond flour
1/2 tsp chili powder
1/2 tsp garlic powder
1/2 tsp cumin
1/4 tsp paprika
1/4 tsp sea salt
1 large egg, beaten
1/2 cup mozzarella cheese, shredded

Directions:
Preheat the oven to 350° F. Line a baking sheet with parchment paper.

In a large bowl, mix together the almond flour and spices.

Add the egg and mix using a hand mixer, until a crumbly dough forms.

In a small bowl, microwave the mozzarella until it's melted and easy to stir (alternatively, you can melt it using a double broiler on the stove). Add to the dough mixture and knead/squeeze with your hands until well incorporated. If it stops incorporating before it's fully mixed, you can reheat it for 15-20 seconds again before kneading more.

Place the dough between two large pieces of parchment paper. Use a rolling pin to roll out very thin, about 1/16 in (2 mm) thick.

Cut the dough into triangles and arranged on the parchment lined baking sheet. Bake for 8-12 minutes, until golden and firm. The chips may release some sizzling oil on the top - just pat dry with a paper towel. They will crisp up as they cool.

61. PUMPKIN SPICE KETO FAT BOMB RECIPE

Prep time: 10 minutes

Ingredients:

1/2 cup coconut oil

3/4 cup pumpkin puree

1/3 cup golden flax

1 tsp cinnamon or I used 2 drops cinnamon bark vitality essential oil

1/2 tsp nutmeg

1/4 tsp sea salt

1/4 cup confectioner's Swerve or 1/3 tsp stevia or to taste

Directions:

Mix all the ingredients in a bowl and place in the freezer for 30 minutes. Roll into balls and place on a plate. Let the balls sit in the refrigerator for 1 hours before eating. Keeps for a week or longer in the freezer.

62. EASY CHEESY ZUCCHINI GRATIN

Ingredients:
4 cups sliced raw zucchini
1 small onion, peeled and sliced thin
salt and pepper to taste
1 1/2 cups shredded pepper jack cheese
2 tbsp butter
1/2 tsp garlic powder
1/2 cup heavy whipping cream

Instructions:
Preheat oven to 375° F.
Grease a 9×9 or equivalent oven-proof pan.
Overlap 1/3 of the zucchini and onion slices in the pan, then season with salt and pepper and sprinkle with 1/2 cup of shredded cheese.
Repeat two more times until you have three layers and have used up all of the zucchini, onions, and shredded cheese.
Combine the garlic powder, butter, and heavy cream in a microwave safe dish.
Heat for one minute or until the butter has melted. Stir.
Gently pour the butter and cream mixture over the zucchini layers.
Bake at 375° F for about 45 minutes, or until the liquid has thickened and the top is golden brown.
Serve warm.

63. KETO SNACKS

Total time: 25 minutes

Ingredients:
4–6 eggs
1 avocado
¼ tsp sea salt
¼ tsp pepper
¼ tsp garlic
¼ tsp chili powder
¼ tsp cumin
¼ tsp smoked paprika, optional*
2 tbsp cilantro

Directions:
In a medium pot, add eggs and cover with water until fully submerged.
Bring to a boil, then remove from heat and cover for 12–13 minutes.
Fill a large bowl with ice water and, using a slotted spoon, gently place eggs in the bowl, allowing eggs to chill for 5 minutes.
Remove outer casing from eggs and slice in half lengthwise, removing the yolk.
Add the yolk, along with the avocado and spices to a bowl, mixing together until well combined.
Add the mixture to the egg halves.
Drizzle with lime juice and top with cilantro.

64. BLACKBERRY-NUT FAT BOMBS

Ingredients:
2 oz macadamia nuts, crushed
4 oz neufchatel cheese (cream cheese)
1 cup blackberries
3 tbsp mascarpone cheese
1 cup coconut oil
1 cup coconut butter
1/2 tsp vanilla extract
1/2 tsp lemon juice
stevia to taste

Directions:
Crush the macadamia nuts and press into the bottom of a baking dish or mold. Bake 5 to 7 minutes at 325 F, or until golden brown.
Remove from the oven and allow to cool slightly.
Spread a layer of softened cream cheese over the nut "crust."
In a bowl, mix together blackberries, mascarpone cheese, coconut oil, coconut butter, vanilla, lemon juice and sweetener (optional) until smooth.
Pour mixture over the cream cheese layer. Freeze for 30 minutes to an hour. Remove and store in the fridge.

65. BUFFALO KETO CHICKEN TENDERS

Prep time: 10 minutes
Cook time: 30 minutes
Total time: 40 minutes

Ingredients:
1 lb chicken breast tenders
1 cup almond flour
1 large egg
1 tbsp heavy whipping cream
6 oz Buffalo sauce
salt & pepper

Instructions:
Preheat oven to 350°.
Season chicken tenders with salt and pepper. Season the almond flour generously with salt and pepper.
Beat 1 egg together with 1 tablespoon of heavy cream.
Dip each tender first in the egg wash and then into the seasoned almond flour. We like to place the tenders in a Tupperware container with the almond flour and shake to coat. A Ziploc bag also works well.
Place tenders on a lightly greased baking sheet. Bake for 30 minutes. If they are not as crispy as you would like you can additionally broil them for 2-3 minutes.

Allow tenders to cool for 5 minutes and then place them in a tupperware container, add the buffalo sauce and shake to coat. Gently shaking is best to prevent the batter from falling off.

66. COCONUT KETO MILK

Prep time: 2 minutes
Cook time: 3 minutes
Total time: 5 minutes

Ingredients:
½ cup filtered water
½ cup coconut milk
2 tbsp unsalted butter (grass-fed)
1 tbsp coconut oil or MCT oil
2 tbsp unsweetened cocoa powder
¼ tsp vanilla extract
dash cinnamon
1-2 teaspoons Erythritol –(optional)

Directions:
In a medium sized pot (if using hand blender) or a small pot (if using blender), bring water and coconut milk to a boil.
Remove from heat.
Add the rest of the ingredients into the coconut milk and water.
Blend using a hand blender (like the ones for soups) or pour the mixture into a blender and blend till frothy.

67. KETO CHEESE MEATBALLS

Prep time: 10 minutes
Cook time: 10 minutes
Total time: 20 minutes

Ingredients:
500 g ground beef
100 g cheese, mozzarella works best, but cheddar is fine
3 tbsp Parmesan cheese
1 tsp garlic Powder
1/2 tsp salt
1/2 tsp pepper

Directions:
Cut the cheese into cubes (1cm by 1cm).
Mix the dry ingredients with the ground beef.
Wrap the cubes of cheese in the meat (500g should make about 9 balls).
Pan fry the meatballs (cover with a lid to capture the heat all around). Fingers crossed the cheese doesn't spill.

68. COCONUT BOOSTERS RECIPE

Total time: 65 minutes

Ingredients:

1 cup coconut oil

1/2 cup chia seeds

1 tsp vanilla extract

1 tbsp honey

1/4 cup unsweetened coconut flakes

Directions:

Using a hand mixer, combine all ingredients together in a bowl.

Spoon into muffin cups/muffin tins and freeze for an hour.

Sprinkle with extra coconut flakes if desired.

69. BAKED MEATBALLS RECIPE

Total time: 15 minutes

Ingredients:
1 lb beef
½ lb of both: lamb and bison
⅓ cup raw, smoked goat cheese
¼ cup of: fresh parsley, fresh basil and oregano, all finely chopped
1-2 tbsp melted coconut oil
1 tsp sea salt
1 tsp pepper
1 tsp onion powder
2 eggs
1 tbsp cassava flour

Directions:
Preheat oven to 375 F.
Line two baking sheets with parchment paper and set aside.
Add all ingredients to a large bowl and, using your hands, mix until well combined.
Roll into small meatballs and place on baking sheets.
Bake for 12-15 minutes or until internal temperature reaches 165 F.

70. GOAT CHEESE & ARTICHOKE DIP RECIPE

Total time: 5 minutes

Ingredients:
14-oz can artichoke hearts, drained
1 lb chévre goat cheese
2 tbsp olive oil
2 tsp lemon juice
1 garlic clove, minced
½ cup pecorino romano, grated
1 tbsp parsley
1 tsp chives
½ tbsp basil
½ tsp sea salt
½ tsp black pepper
Dash of cayenne pepper (optional)

Directions:
In a food processor, mix all ingredients except the pecorino romano until well incorporated and creamy. Top with freshly-grated pecorino romano.

71. LOW-CARB INDIAN SAMOSAS

Prep time: 25 minutes
Cook time: 17 minutes
Total time: 37 minutes

Ingredients:
1 tbsp butter preferably grass-fed
6 oz cauliflower finely chopped
1 medium onion, about 4 oz
3/4 tsp salt (or to taste)
1 tbsp fresh ginger root, minced
1/2 tsp coriander ground
1 tsp garam masala ground
1 tsp cumin ground
1/4 tsp cumin seeds whole
1/8-1/4 tsp red chili flakes
1/4 cup fresh cilantro chopped

Dough:
3/4 cup super-fine almond flour
1/4 tsp cumin
1/2 tsp salt
8 oz part-skim mozzarella cheese, finely shredded

Directions:
For the filling:

Preheat a large skillet over medium heat. Add butter. When butter has melted and stopped foaming, add the cauliflower and onions.

Sprinkle the salt over the vegetables.Cook, stirring occasionally, until the edges have started to brown and the vegetables are cooked through.

Stir in ginger root, coriander, garam masala, ground cumin, cumin seeds, and chili flakes. Stir for 1-2 minutes to allow the spices to toast. Turn off the heat.

Stir in the cilantro. Taste and adjust seasoning. Add salt to taste.

Preheat oven to 375° F. Have a rolling pin, 2 pieces of parchment, and a baking sheet available.

For the dough:

Set up a double boiler. I use a large sauce pan with about 1 1/2-2 inches of water in it and a medium mixing bowl that fits on top.

Bring the water in the lower part of the double boiler to a simmer over high heat. Once it is simmering, turn heat to low.

Meanwhile, place the almond flour, cumin, salt, and mozzarella in the top part of the double boiler. Stir together.

Place the bowl containing the almond flour mixture over the simmering water. Be careful not to burn yourself with the hot bowl or with steam escaping. I use a silicone mitten to hold the bowl.

Stirring the mixture constantly, heat until the mozzarella cheese melts and the mixture forms a dough.

Turn the dough out onto one of the pieces of parchment and knead a few times to equally distribute the ingredients. Shape the dough into a thick rectangle and cover with the second sheet of parchment. Roll dough into a rectangle about 8 inches wide by 16 inches long.

Cut the dough rectangle in half lengthwise, then in half cross-wise. Then cut each of the four sections in half crosswise to form 8 four-inch squares.

To assemble:

Spoon the filling onto the center of each square, dividing it equally among the squares. Fold the squares on the diagonal to form triangles and pinch the edges closed. Place one of the pieces of parchment used to roll out the dough onto a baking sheet, then place the samosas on the sheet.

Make fork holes in each samosa to provide a place for steam to release. Bake for 14-17 minutes or until golden-brown.

72. CHOCOLATE AVOCADO PUDDING

Total time: 5 minutes

Ingredients:

1/4 cup unsweetened cocoa powder

1 medium avocado

10 drops liquid Stevia

1/2 tsp vanilla extract

1 tsp pink salt

Directions:

Remove the pit from the avocado and place in a mixing bowl.

Add cocoa powder, stevia, and vanilla extract and mix with a fork until a pudding is formed. You can gently use a hand mixer also, but a fork does the job.

Top with pink sea salt.

73. LOADED HASSELBACK ZUCCHINI

Prep time: 10 minutes
Cook time: 15 minutes
Total time: 25 minutes

Ingredients:
3 medium zucchini squash
about 6-8 oz of your favorite cheese
3-4 tbsp sour cream
3 slices of crumbled cooked bacon
2-3 tbsp chopped green onion
salt and pepper, to taste

Notes: For this recipe you can use sliced cheese (pre-sliced or sliced fresh off the block) or shredded cheese. Both work great, but I find using slices the easiest. I cut my slices off the block, then cut each slice in half. You can even skip the stuffing portion altogether and whisk together a simple nacho-style cheddar cheese sauce to pour over each zucchini. Anything goes when it comes to cheese.

Directions:
Preheat oven to 425° F.
Wash and dry zucchini, and slice off the ends.
Line up a chopstick on both sides of the squash and slice until you hit the stick.

Start at one end and keep slicing into discs (granted - connected discs since we don't want to cut all the way through the squash) until you've reached the other end. Repeat for remaining squash.

Resist the urge to play the zucchini accordion-style when you're done.

Slice each zucchini in half so you have 6 mini hasselbacks.

Line a baking sheet with foil, then arrange your zukes on top.

Next, stuff cheese between each tasty little zucchini disc.

Season with salt and pepper if desired and top with another sheet of foil.

Pinch along the sides to make a foil pouch.

The foil pouch will not only help the zucchini cook quicker by steaming the squash, but will also keep the cheese melty and prevent it from browning.

Bake at 425° F for 15-20 minutes.

Allow to rest/steam covered in foil for an additional 5.

Top with sour cream, bacon, and green onion and dig in.

74. GUILTLESS GARLIC PARMESAN WINGS

Total time: 35 minutes

Ingredients:

12 chicken wings

1½ tbsp avocado oil

1 tbsp garlic powder

½ cup parmesan, grated

½ cup pecorino romano, grated

1 tsp salt

1 tsp pepper

Directions:

Preheat oven to 350 F.

Line a baking sheet with parchment and set aside.

Mix spices and cheeses in a bowl.

Coat the wings in oil.

Dip wings in mixture.

Bake for 30 minutes.

75. EGGPLANT ROLLATINI RECIPE

Total time: 1 hour

Ingredients:
2 large eggplants, sliced lengthwise
½ tsp sea salt
½ tsp black pepper
1–1½ cups marinara sauce
2 large eggs
3 cups spinach
1 package goat feta (4 oz)
1 tsp dried oregano
1 tsp parsley
1 tsp dried basil
2 cups pecorino romano, grated
1 cup raw sheep cheese, grated

Directions:
Preheat oven to 450 F.
While the oven is heating up, cut the ends off of the two eggplants and then slice lengthwise.
Place the eggplant slices on a baking sheet lined with parchment paper and sprinkle with salt and pepper.
Bake for 12–15 minutes, remove and allow to cool.
Reduce heat to 400 F.
In a medium bowl, mix the eggs, goat cheese, spinach, oregano, parsley, basil, 1 cup pecorino

romano, ½ cup raw sheep cheese, salt and pepper, mixing until well combined.

In a 9x13 baking dish, add ¾ cup marinara.

Place ¼ cup cheese mixture onto one end of the sliced eggplant, then roll it up and transfer to baking dish, continuing until baking dish is full.

Cover with remaining marinara and cheese.

Bake for 25 minutes and allow to cool for 10 minutes before serving

76. MEATBALLS

Prep time: 15 minutes
Cook time: 15 minutes
Total time: 30 minutes

Ingredients:
1/4 cup grated Parmesan cheese
1/4 cup golden flaxseed meal
1 tbsp Italian seasoning
3/4 tsp sea salt
1/2 tsp black pepper
1/4 cup unsweetened coconut milk beverage (or any milk of choice)
3 tbsp onion, grated
1 large egg
3 cloves garlic, minced
2 tbsp fresh parsley chopped
1 lb ground beef
3/4 cup marinara sauce

Directions:
Preheat the oven to 425° F. Line a baking sheet with parchment paper or foil (grease if using foil).
In a large bowl, stir together the grated Parmesan cheese, golden flaxseed meal, Italian seasoning, sea salt, and black pepper.

Whisk in the milk, grated onion, egg, garlic, and fresh parsley. Let the mixture sit for a couple of minutes.

Mix in the ground beef using your hands, until just incorporated (don't over-mix to avoid tough meatballs).

Form the mixture into 1-inch balls and place on the lined baking sheet (a small cookie scoop works well for this. If using your hands, use a gentle touch and don't pack the meatballs too tightly).

Bake for 10-12 minutes, until the meatballs are barely done (if you want them more golden, you can place them under the broiler for a couple of minutes).

Top each meatball with marinara sauce. Return to the oven and bake for 3-5 minutes, until the sauce is hot and meatballs are cooked through. Garnish with additional fresh parsley.

HOW TO STORE FOOD SAFELY AND PREVENT FOODBORNE ILLNESSES

Some foods are more susceptible to harmful pathogens than others, like milk and dairy products, eggs, beef, pork, lamb, poultry, fish, shellfish, baked potatoes, cooked rice, sprouts, sliced melons, cut melons, untreated garlic, and oil mixtures and many, many more.

Prevention of foodborne illnesses should be a primary focus of every kitchen in America. Each year, millions of people get sick from unsafe foods and over 30% of the suspected cases of foodborne illness happens at home.

Here are the five most common risk factors causing foodborne illnesses as identified by the CDC (Centers for Disease Control):

1. Purchasing food from unsafe food sources.

2. Failing to cook food adequately.

3. Holding food at incorrect temperatures.

4. Using contaminated equipment.

5. Practicing poor personal hygiene.

You can help to keep your holiday foods safe by controlling FAT TOM. What is FAT TOM? FAT TOM is the six conditions in which pathogens grow. Taking care of these six conditions helps prevent outbreaks of foodborne illnesses.

F = Food. Pathogens need a source of energy.

A = Acidity. Foods that contain little or no acidity are where pathogens grown best.

T = Temperature. Pathogens grow best in food held between 41°F and 135°F. This is known as the "danger zone."

T = time. Pathogens need time to grow. After four hours, food left in the danger zone will grow a high enough legal of pathogens to make someone sick.

O = Oxygen. Some pathogens need oxygen to grow while some others grow where there is no oxygen.

M = Moisture. Pathogens need moisture in food to grow.

As you can see, these items are easy to follow. Become familiar with these tips and use your new knowledge to keep food safe and thereby help to keep your family and guests safe.

When you are thinking about starting a long-term food storage program, there many things to consider.

First off, what are your food storage goals? A common guideline is to start with a three-month supply of foods you normally eat, and then build up a one-year supply of longer-term foods.

What IS long-term food storage? This concept is basically to have a supply of food that can sustain your family for one year in case of a long-lasting emergency situation. These bulk foods tend to have long shelf lives and when combined with a few other ingredients can make a wide variety of meals. Some of the most common foods stored are wheat, oats, rice, legumes, powdered milk, oil, salt, yeast, etc. Basically, the staple foods of any diet.

How much should you store? While there are basic food storage calculators out there to help you along the way, they aren't necessarily exactly right for every situation. Here are some do's and don'ts that can help you as you get started with your family's personal plan.

Food Storage Do's:

- DO get a partner to work with you, share ideas, and motivate you.

- DO learn how to actually USE the foods that you are storing.

- DO buy the necessary kitchen appliances to help you use the foods.

- DO include the foods you store as part of your everyday cooking.

- DO be adventurous and try new recipes.

- DO start small and work your way up to a full year supply.

- DO make sure to have an emergency plan in place.

- DO expand your food storage to include other things once you get the basics down.

- DO educate yourself in other aspects of emergency preparedness such as alternative heating/cooking methods.

Food Storage Don'ts:

- DON'T get overwhelmed and just give up completely.

- DON'T store foods that your family hates just because the calculator says to.

- DON'T think that cooking with these foods is fattening and unhealthy.

- DON'T think that using bulk foods and cooking from scratch is really inconvenient.

- DON'T get too crazy about figuring out how to cook without electricity when you are just getting started.

- DON'T buy everything all at once and kill your budget.

- DON'T try to get your family to change their diet completely overnight.

- DON'T be too anxious to buy things that you don't wait for good sales.

- DON'T focus too much on long-term items and neglect to store some basic foods you use on a regular basis.

KETO DIET FOR BEGINNERS

A COMPLETE KETOGENIC DIET FOR BEGINNERS

INTRODUCTION

In order to rapidly burn fat using the body's natural metabolism, consider a ketogenic diet plan. Nutrition has the strongest effect on the body's production of important hormones, which regulate metabolism and allow the body to burn fat for energy while retaining muscle mass, with little need for excessive exercise.

CHAPTER ONE

KETO DIETING

What Is the Keto Diet?

The Keto diet involves going long spells on extremely low (no higher than 30g per day) to almost zero grams per day of carbs and increasing your fats to a really high level (to the point where they may make up as much as 65% of your daily macronutrients intake). The idea behind this is to get your body into a state of ketosis. In this state of ketosis, the body is supposed to be more inclined to use fat for energy- and research says it does just this. Depleting your carbohydrate/glycogen liver stores and then moving onto fat for fuel means you should end up being shredded.

Calculate your required maintenance level of daily calories...

(if you are looking to drop quickly, then use 13- I would not advise this, if you want a more level drop in body fat use 15, and if you are going to actually attempt to maintain or possibly put on some lean muscle mass, then use 17)

Body weight in pounds x 15= a

Protein for the day 1g per body weight in pounds= b

Bx4=c (c= number of calories allotted to your daily protein allowance)

a-c= d (d= amount of calories to be allotted to fat intake)

D/9= grams per day of fat to be consumed.

The end calculation should leave you with a very high number for your fat intake.

Now, for those of you wondering about energy levels... Especially for training because there are no carbs, with there being such a high amount of fat in the diet you will feel quite full and the fat is a very good fuel source for your body (one adaptation that I have made is to actually have a nice fish fillet about an hour before I train and I find it gives me enough energy to get through my workout).

I am aware of the arguments made to not have fats 2-3 hrs otherwise of training. While I won't have fats 2-3 hrs after training as I want quick absorption and blood flow, then I see no issue with slowing everything down before training so my body has access to a slow-digesting energy source.

Continuing with general guidelines...

There are some that say to have a 30g carb intake immediately after training- just enough to fill liver glycogen levels. And then there are those that say that having even as much as that may push you out of ketosis- the state you are trying to maintain.

During my carb up period- for the sake of those who would like to know if you can get in shape and still eat the things you want (in moderation)- for the first six weeks, I will be relaxed about what I eat in this period but then the following six weeks I only eat clean carbs.

I also like to make sure that the first workout of the week- as in a Monday morning workout- is a nice, long full hour of work so I start cutting into the liver glycogen already.

Plan menus and snacks at least a week ahead of time, so you aren't caught with only high-carb meal choices. Research keto recipes online; there are quite a few good ones to choose from. Immerse yourself in the keto lifestyle, find your favorite recipes, and stick with them.

There are a few items that are staples of a keto diet. Be sure to have these on hand:

• Eggs - Used in omelets, quiches (yes, heavy cream is

legal on keto!), hard-boiled as a snack, low carb pizza crust, and more; if you like eggs, you have a great chance of success on this diet

• Bacon - Do I need a reason? Breakfast, salad garnish, burger topper, BLT's (no bread of course; try a BLT in a bowl, tossed in mayo)

• Cream cheese - Dozens of recipes, pizza crusts, main dishes, desserts

• Shredded cheese - Sprinkle over taco meat in a bowl, made into tortilla chips in the microwave, salad toppers, low-carb pizza and enchiladas

• Lots of romaine and spinach - Fill up on the green veggies; have plenty on hand for a quick salad when hunger pangs hit

• EZ-Sweetz liquid sweetener - Use a couple of drops in place of sugar; this artificial sweetener is the most natural and easiest to use that I've found

• Cauliflower - Fresh or frozen bags; you can eat this low-carb veggie by itself, tossed in olive oil and baked, mashed in fake potatoes, chopped/shredded and used in place of rice under main dishes, in low-carb and keto pizza crusts, and much more

• Frozen chicken tenders - Have a large bag on hand;

thaw quickly and grill, saute, mix with veggies and top with garlic sauce in a low-carb flatbread, use in chicken piccata, chicken alfredo, tacos, enchiladas, Indian Butter chicken, and more

• Ground beef - Make a big burger and top with all sorts of things from cheese, to sauteed mushrooms, to grilled onions... or crumble and cook with taco seasoning and use in provolone cheese taco shells; throw in a dish with lettuce, avocado, cheese, sour cream for a tortilla-less taco salad

• Almonds (plain or flavored) - These are a tasty and healthy snack; however, be sure to count them as you eat, because the carbs DO add up. Flavors include habanero, coconut, salt and vinegar, and more.

The keto plan is a versatile and interesting way to lose weight, with lots of delicious food choices. Keep these 10 items stocked in your fridge, freezer, and larder, and you'll be ready to throw together some delicious keto meals and snacks at a moment's notice

SO WHAT FOODS ARE ENCOURAGED?

Some of the best-tasting, most fulfilling foods are part of this plan, including lean meats like beef and chicken; healthy sources of protein and high-quality fats like eggs, butter, olive oil, coconut oil, and avocado. Also, delicious, leafy, green vegetables like kale, chard, and spinach, as well as cruciferous vegetables like broccoli, cabbage, and cauliflower.

These foods can be combined with seeds, nuts, sprouts, and a wide range of other amazing foods that lead to incredible health benefits that give your body the protein, healthy fats, and nutrients it needs while providing metabolism-boosting meals for easy cooking at home or on the go.

WHAT FOODS SHOULD BE LIMITED?

On a ketogenic diet plan, the main foods to avoid are those high in carbohydrates, sugars, and the wrong types of fats. These foods can be toxic to the body and create excess glucose levels that the body turns into stored fat. These foods increase the levels of insulin and blood sugar in the body, and will prevent fat loss even if you are putting a lot of energy into exercise. To avoid these foods, limit your intake of grains, processed foods, vegetable oils (canola, corn, soybean, etc.), milk, margarine, and other high-carbohydrate, high-sugar foods.

WHAT ARE THE BENEFITS OF A KETOGENIC DIET PLAN?

- Burn Stored Fat - By cutting out the high levels of carbohydrates in your diet that produce glucose (sugar), a ketogenic diet plan tells your body to burn stored fat by converting this fat into fatty acids and ketone bodies in the liver. These ketone bodies replace the role of glucose that was being filled by carbohydrates in the diet. This leads to a rapid reduction in the amount of fat stored in the body.

- Retain Muscle Mass - By including the right fats in your diet, a ketogenic diet plan provides your body with the energy it needs to convert existing fat stores into useful sugars and ketones (through gluconeogenesis), which are an essential source of energy for the brain, muscles, and heart. This has the added benefit of preserving muscle mass, because the healthy fat in the diet gives the body the energy it needs without having to tap into muscle protein to create more sugar. This creates the best of both worlds – you burn fat while maintaining muscle mass!

- Eliminate Excess Fat - Even better, if your body

creates too many ketone bodies by converting existing fat, it will simply eliminate those ketones as a waste product, which means you will basically pee out any unwanted body fat!

- Reduce Appetite - Lastly, by regulating the powerful metabolic hormones in your body, a ketogenic diet plan will actually reduce your appetite. By lowering your body's insulin resistance and increasing ketones, you will actually feel less hungry on this diet, which is an amazing advantage over other low-calorie, carbohydrate-rich weight loss diets that come with the expectation of lingering hunger.

Start burning fat today without more exercise! Take control of your metabolism naturally by adopting a ketogenic diet plan. Your body was designed for this style of nutrition. Your metabolic state can be optimized by consuming the (delicious) foods that our genetic forefathers thrived on, and this does not include carbohydrate-rich, processed foods loaded with sugars and bad fats. It involves a luxurious and fulfilling diet based on bountiful foods from paleolithic times, including lean meats, vegetables, nuts and seeds, and healthy fats that your body will thank you for

CHAPTER TWO

KETOGENIC DIETS

Some would argue that only the first "phase" of the Atkins Diet is "ketogenic", but it's very clear that this element is central to the whole diet. There are many other diets of this type with different names and claims but, if they talk about severely restricting the intake of carbohydrates, then they're probably forms of a ketogenic diet. The process of "ketosis" is quite complicated and would take some time to describe but, in essence, it works because cutting down on carbs restricts the amount of blood glucose available to trigger the "insulin response". Without a triggering of the glucose-insulin response, some hormonal changes take place which cause the body to start burning its stores of fat as energy. This also has the interesting effect of causing your brain to be fuelled by what are known as "ketone bodies" (hence "ketogenic") rather than the usual glucose. The whole process is really quite fascinating and I recommend that you read up on it.

Controversy

All forms of ketogenic diet are controversial. Most of the debate surrounds the issue of cholesterol and whether ketogenic diets increase or decrease the levels of HDL "good" cholesterol and/or increase or decrease LDL "bad" cholesterol. The number of scientific studies is increasing year on year and it is certainly possible to point to strong cases on both sides of the argument. My conclusion (and this is only my opinion) is that one could equally make the case that a carbohydrate-laden diet has negative effects on cholesterol and I think that, on balance, a ketogenic-type diet is more healthy than a carbohydrate-heavy one. Interestingly, there isn't so much controversy about whether ketogenic diets work or not (it's widely accepted that they do); it's mostly about how they work and whether if that is good/bad/indifferent from a health perspective.

1. Low carb (ketogenic) diets deplete the healthy glycogen (the storage form of glucose) stores in your muscles and liver. When you deplete glycogen stores, you also dehydrate, often causing the scale to drop significantly in the first week or two of the diet. This is usually interpreted as fat loss when it's actually mostly from dehydration and muscle loss. By the way, this is one of the reasons that low carb diets are so popular at the moment - there is a quick initial, but deceptive drop in scale weight.

Glycogenesis (formation of glycogen) occurs in the

liver and muscles when adequate quantities of carbohydrates are consumed - very little of this happens on a low carb diet.

Glycogenolysis (breakdown of glycogen) occurs when glycogen is broken down to form glucose for use as fuel.

2. Depletion of muscle glycogen causes you to fatigue easily, and makes exercise and movement uncomfortable. Research indicates that muscle fatigue increases in almost direct proportion to the rate of depletion of muscle glycogen. Bottom line is that you don't feel energetic and you exercise and move less (often without realizing it) which is not good for caloric expenditure and basal metabolic rate (metabolism).

3. Depletion of muscle glycogen leads to muscle atrophy (loss of muscle). This happens because muscle glycogen (broken down to glucose) is the fuel of choice for muscles during movement. There is always a fuel mix, but without muscle glycogen, the muscle fibers that contract, even at rest to maintain muscle tone, contract less when glycogen is not immediately available in the muscle. Depletion of muscle glycogen also causes you to exercise and move less than normal, which leads to muscle loss and the inability to maintain adequate muscle tone.

Also, in the absence of adequate carbohydrates for fuel, the body initially uses protein (muscle) and fat. the initial phase of muscle depletion is rapid, caused by the use of easily-accessed muscle protein for direct metabolism or for conversion to glucose (gluconeogenesis) for fuel. Eating excess protein does not prevent this because there is a caloric deficit.

When insulin levels are chronically too low, as they may be in very low carb diets, catabolism (breakdown) of muscle protein increases, and protein synthesis stops.

4. Loss of muscle causes a decrease in your basal metabolic rate (metabolism). Metabolism happens in the muscle. Less muscle and muscle tone means a slower metabolism, which means fewer calories burned 24 hours-a-day.

5. Your muscles and skin lack tone and are saggy. Saggy muscles don't look good, cause saggy skin, and cause you to lose a healthy, vibrant look (even if you've also lost fat).

6. Some proponents of low-carb diets recommend avoiding carbohydrates such as bread, pasta, potatoes, carrots, etc. because they are high on the glycemic index - causing a sharp rise in insulin. Certain carbohydrates have always been, and will always be

the bad guys: candy, cookies, baked goods with added sugar, sugared drinks, processed/refined white breads, pastas, and rice, and any foods with added sugar.These are not good for health or weight loss; carbohydrates such as fruits, vegetables, legumes, whole grain breads and pastas, and brown rice are good for health and weight loss. Just like carbohydrates should be eaten in moderation. Large volumes of any proteins, fats, or carbohydrates are not conducive to weight loss and health.

The effect of high-glycemic foods is often exaggerated. It does matter, but to a smaller degree than is often portrayed. Also,the total glycemic effect of foods is influenced by the quantity of that food that you eat in a sitting. Smaller meals have a lower overall glycemic effect. Also, we usually eat several types of food at the same time, thereby reducing the average glycemic index of the meal, if higher glycemic foods are eaten.

Also, glycemic index values can be misleading because they are based on a standard 50 grams of carbohydrate consumed.

It wouldn't take many candy bars to get that, but it would take four cups of carrots. Do you usually eat four cups of carrots in a meal?

Regular exercisers and active people also are less affected by higher glycemic foods because many of the carbohydrates comsumed are immediately used to replenish glycogen stores in the liver and muscle.

By the way, if you're interested in lowering insulin levels, there is a great way to do that - exercise and activity.

7. Much of the weight loss on a low-carb, high-protein diet, especially in the first few weeks, is actually because of dehydration and muscle loss.

8. The percentage of people that re-gain the weight they've lost with most methods of weight loss is high, but it's even higher with low-carb, high-protein diets. This is primarily due to four factors:

• You have lost muscle. With that comes a slower metabolism, which means fewer calories are burned 24 hours-a-day. A loss of muscle during the process of losing weight is almost a guarantee for re-gaining the lost weight, and more.

• You re-gain the healthy fluids lost because of glycogen depletion.

• It's difficult to maintain that type of diet long-term.

• You have not made a change to a long-term healthy

lifestyle.

9. Eating too much fat is just not healthy. I know you've heard of people whose blood levels of cholesterol and triglycerides have decreased while on a low-carb, high-protein diet. This often happens with weight loss, but it doesn't continue when you're on a diet high in fat.

There are literally reams of research over decades that clearly indicate that an increase in consumption of animal products and/or saturated fat leads to increased incidence of heart disease, strokes, gall stones, kidney stones, arthritic symptoms, certain cancers, etc. For example, in comparing countries with varying levels of meat consumption, there is a direct relationship between the volume of meat consumption in a country and the incidence of digestive cancers (stomach, intestines, rectal, etc.).

CHAPTER THREE

TYPES OF KETOGENIC DIETS

A ketogenic diet is a high-fat low-carbohydrate diet with adequate protein thrown in the meal. It is further divided into three types and, depending on one's daily calorie needs, the percentage differs. Diets are often prepared on a ratio level such as 4:1 or 2:1 with the first number indicating the total fat amount in the diet compared to the protein and carbohydrates combined in each meal.

Standard - SKD

The first diet is the Standard or the SKD and is designed for individuals who are not active or lead a sedentary lifestyle. The meal plan limits the dieter to eat a net of 20-50 grams of carbohydrates. Fruits or vegetables that are starchy are restricted from the diet. In order for the diet to be effective, one must strictly follow the meal plan. Butter, vegetable oil, and heavy creams are used heavily to replace carbohydrates in the diet.

Targeted - TKD

The TKD is less strict than the SKD and allows one to consume carbohydrates, though only in a certain portion or amount which will not impact the ketosis that one is currently in. The TKD diet helps dieters that perform some level of exercise or workout.

Cyclical - CKD

The CKD is preferable for those who are into weight training or do intensive exercises and is not for beginners as it requires the person undergoing the diet to stick to a SKD meal plan for five days in a week's time and eating/loading up on carbohydrates on the next two days. It is important that dieters follow the strict regimen to ensure that their diet is successful.

Ketones happen as a result of the body burning fat for energy versus glucose. A ketogenic diet refers to one that is low in carbohydrates, which will allow the body to break down fat faster in order to metabolize ketones.

Foods or ingredients that allow the body to make ketones are medium-chain triglycerides like:

• MCT oil

• Grass-fed butter

• Coconut oil

The important factor about ketones is that they help rid you of migraines.

HERE ARE THE TOP SEVEN WAYS KETONES SQUASH MIGRAINES:

1: Decreased Migraine Frequency

In recent studies, scientists have found that the ketogenic diet significantly reduced the frequency of migraines in 90% of patients. This completely dwarfs the effects of migraine drugs.

2: Glutamate Inhibition

Glutamate is found in both epilepsy and migraine patients. Medications that work in epilepsy (anti-seizure drugs) also block glutamate production. These drugs have been used to treat migraines as well. Since about 500 BC, ketones have worked to help prevent seizures, but the ketogenic diet has only been popular for the last century.

3: Processed Food

I have said many times that processed foods are bad for you, especially if you suffer with migraines. "Food-like products" are filled with preservatives, chemicals, and other triggers that could be affecting your migraine symptoms. Any diet that removes those processed foods, including the ketogenic diet, would be a good step to controlling migraine symptoms.

4: Saturated Fats

Several studies have debunked the great saturated fat myth. There are plenty of saturated fats (and other healthy fats) in a ketogenic diet, which has been found to reduce bad cholesterol and help the body produce serotonin and vitamin D, both of which help prevent migraines.

5: Hunger vs. Weight Management

Hunger is a major migraine trigger, so is weight gain/obesity. Some studies have found that weight gain and/or obesity increases the risk of migraines by 81%. Ketones help reduce hunger, while controlling insulin problems, promoting weight loss, and regulating glucose levels in the blood. Weight loss and sugar control are well-known benefits from adding MCT or coconut oil to your diet. Now, as you can see, they will help control migraines by helping you feel nutritionally satisfied, more energetic, improve cognitive functioning, and lose fat.

6: Oxidative Stress

A recent study found that oxidative stress is tied to migraine triggers. In response to these findings, a new migraine medication has come out which blocks the peptide released during oxidative stress. This drug also prevents glutamate release, another migraine trigger. You don't need to depend on medication, however. A ketogenic diet will do both for you, which indicates that ketones can not only treat migraine symptoms, but also determine the root cause.

7: MCT Oil

Research has found that Alzheimer's patients respond favorably to MCT (medium-chain triglyceride) oil, especially with regards to memory recall. Like Alzheimer's, migraine patients have white-matter brain lesions on their scans. Research in both diseases has found that ketones may help increase metabolism in the brain, even when oxidative stress and glucose intolerance is present.

Our minds and bodies need glucose and/or ketones to function and survive. We store about 24 hours' worth of sugar in our bodies, but we'd all die of hypoglycemia if not for the ketones. Metabolizing ketones from fat leaves our body in a healthy state of ketosis.

Migraines indicate that the brain is not metabolizing glucose into energy properly, so the logical response would be to add ketones. In addition to migraine pain symptoms, the ketogenic diet can help reduce:

• Brain fog

• Oxidative stress

• Brain lesions

A ketogenic diet can also help:

• Block glutamate (a major trigger)

• Eliminate processed foods (a major trigger)

• Add more saturated and healthy fats to your diet

• Control your weight

• Reduce oxidative stress

• Improve cognitive functioning

Chronic migraine headaches can control your life. The pain can be unbearable, relentless, and incredibly overwhelming, leaving you depressed, scared, and many times, alone.

CHAPTER FOUR

KETOSIS - THE CYCLICAL KETOGENIC DIET BURN

We want to give a clearer picture of what your body will be going through while on the cyclical ketogenic diet. This chapter will focus on ketosis and what benefits it provides you.

Ketosis is a state in which your body goes on a fat-burning autopilot. How's that! The fat that is stored in your body begins to get used as energy, which will allow for weight reduction of fat, not water or muscle.

Many diets promoted are calorie-restriction diets. They help you lose weight, but, most of the weight is in the form of water and muscle. Little fat stores are broken down. This is the problem with a calorie-restrictive eating program. Your metabolism gets slower because your body begins to think it is starving and must slow down the process of losing calories. A slow metabolism equals slower weight loss and faster weight gain!

The cyclical ketogenic diet restricts carbohydrates. By restricting carbohydrates, but maintaining caloric consumption, your body will have only one option of fuel consumption. That is fat; which is what ketosis is. You are essentially turning on your fat-burning machine. Ketones are sent out of your body and fat loss becomes profound. How does this happen? The largest internal organ in your body is the key player. Your liver. The liver has the job of converting fat into ketones. These ketones are then excreted out of the body, promoting weight/fat loss. This is a natural process.

Ketones are created in the liver and are an efficient source of energy for the body. Fatty acids that are broken down from body fat are created in the liver as these ketones. Ketones can only be made present when there is a lack of sugar and glucose in the body. Carbohydrates contain both of these substances. It will always be difficult to lose weight on a high-carbohydrate based diet. On the ketogenic diet, the amount of sugar and glucose is reduced to the point where they are no longer the primary source of fuel to be burned in the bloodstream.

We should take a moment to talk about a couple of myths surrounding the ketogenic diet and whether it is healthy in the long term. Our bodies can perform in the state of ketosis and be healthy. This state of ketosis is a natural occurrence when the body is not using sugar and glucose. The human body has no problem operating in this state naturally. In other words, it is safe to burn the fat.

HOW DO YOU KNOW IF YOU ARE IN A FAT-BURNING STATE?

A simple walk to the drug store can answer that quickly. You can use ketone testing strips to check your level of ketosis. Simply capture a urine sample on the strips and check for a color change. The magic color to look for is a pink to purple result. Check the color scale to see your ketone levels and where you are in the fat-burning zone.

The use of these strips will be your source of the level of ketones being released. This is the gauge by which you will know if you are properly keeping your carbohydrate intake to the necessary level to facilitate ketosis. Don't worry if you are not at the dark purple level. Different people have different levels. Just watch the scale and if you are losing weight, you are pretty much ok!

Here is a word of warning about dehydration. If you are seeing dark purple consistently, please make sure you are drinking enough water. Sometimes the dark purple indicates dehydration. Make sure you keep yourself hydrated properly when on the ketogenic plan.

The fat-burning mechanism associated with ketosis is at the heart of the cyclical ketogenic diet. Restricting carbohydrates and allowing your body the ability to burn those fat reserves will help you achieve your weight loss goals and obtain the body contour you have set goals to have. Get your ketone strips and watch your fat-burning begin.

Eat your veggies (they're the good carbs and won't interfere with your low carb benefits)!

Choose lean meats and eggs (eggs are a great source of protein, as is grass-fed organic meat)

Choose better fats (make sure you eat a regular supply of omega 3 fats amongst your other daily intakes. Saturated fat in moderation is not the danger. Sugar is)

Stay away from sugars and grains (low carbohydrate is less about maligning one particular food group and more about staying away from those sources which your body can't handle in large amounts)!

Athletes and healthy individuals may be able to use limited sugar and/or grains to improve performance but the same basic rules apply elsewhere)

Drink lots of water (we often argue over what groups of food are essential or not, but one we can all agree on is water. You need it and lots of it. Forget food, without water you die fast!)

Be wary of special low-carb foods (there are a great

number of healthy choices here, athletes especially will enjoy easy-to-mix carb-free protein drinks, etc., but as low-carb diets have hit certain food industries hard, expect lots of products that may be lower carb choices but are not healthy. Always remember the low-fat craze where manufacturers swapped saturated fat for lots of sugar...)

Mix your food choices (restricting grains and sugars is a great start but don't fall into the trap of just surviving on the same meat diet day in and day out. Mix your proteins and fats and vegetables to offer a wide variety of healthy options)

Enjoy the diet (just because you stopped eating chips and bread with your meals doesn't mean you have to get bored! There is a limitless supply of sauces, seasonings, meats, eggs, and vegetables that don't require high-carb sugar and corn syrup additives to make great-tasting meals. Get fitter and healthier and enjoy your food while you do. Enjoying bacon once in a while poses little threat. Compare this to downing a fizzy drink with eight spoons of addictive, toxic sugar, and you see the advantages already)

CHAPTER FIVE

LOW-CARB AND KETO DIET FAST FOOD MENU CHOICES

For those who eat low-carb or keto diets, there is almost always something you can eat in every fast food place or restaurant. Plan ahead. Before entering a restaurant, check out their menu and nutrition information online at home or using your smartphone. It's always good to know the safe options before being tempted by menu items you shouldn't have on a low-carb diet.

In order to make it easier to find a quick, keto-friendly option, I've compiled a list of several restaurants and fast food places and those items that I've found to be the lowest carb (and most emotionally satisfying) choices. These are not all perfect options, but when you're stuck with no other choices due to time or location constraints, they'll do in a pinch.

It's a huge help that fast-food places are required to post nutritional content. It gets easier to follow the keto plan every day. The carb count I'm listing is approximate and is NET grams.

In general, there is usually some sort of salad option

anywhere you are. At burger joints, just remove the bun, and many places offer lettuce wraps instead. Chicken shouldn't have breading.

As a side note, it helps to have a knife and fork handy in your car or purse. Big, juicy burgers in tiny pieces of lettuce end up on the table - or in your lap. Small, flimsy fast food plasticware also makes for difficult eating. Pull out your own sturdy utensils and enjoy!

Now for the food choices... here are some pretty obvious general rules to follow:

Skip the bun or wrap

Skip the pasta, potato, or rice

Salads - No croutons. Stick with low-sugar dressing options - Caesar, Blue Cheese, Ranch, Chipotle. Look at the name which may give you a clue, things like "honey" in the honey dijon or "sweet" in the dressing name - these are usually not a good choice. Check the ingredients for items that are higher in carb content.

Chicken - Choose grilled or sauteed. Stay away from any chicken that is breaded.

Ketogenic Diet - Ultimate Fat Loss Diet

In simple terms, it's when you trick your body into using your own BODY FAT as its main energy source instead of carbohydrates. The keto diet is a very popular method of losing fat quickly and efficiently.

The Science Behind It

To get your body into a ketogenic state, you must eat a high-fat diet and low protein with NO carbs or hardly any. The ratio should be around 80% fat and 20% protein. This will be the guideline for the first two days. Once in a ketogenic state, you will have to increase the protein intake and lower fat; the ratio will be around 65% fat, 30% protein, and 5% carbs. Protein is increased to spare muscle tissue. When your body intakes carbohydrates, it causes an insulin spike which means the pancreas releases insulin (helps store glycogen, amino acids, and excess calories as fat) so common sense tells us that if we eliminate carbs, then the insulin will not store excess calories as fat. Perfect.

Now that your body has no carbs as an energy source it must find a new one. Fat. This works out perfectly if you want to lose body fat. The body will break down the body fat and use it as energy instead of carbs. This state is called ketosis. This is the state you want your body to be in, it makes perfect sense if you want to lose body fat while maintaining muscle.

Now to the diet part and how to plan it. You will need

to intake AT LEAST a gram of protein per pound of LEAN MASS. This will help in the recovery and repair of muscle tissue after workouts and such. Remember the ratio? 65% fat and 30% protein. Well, if you weight 150 pounds of lean mass, that means 150g of protein a day, X4 (amount of calories per gram of protein), which is 600 calories. The rest of your calories should come from fat. If your caloric maintenance is 3000, you must eat around 500 less, which would mean that if you need 2500 calories a day, and around 1900 calories must come from fats! You must eat fats to fuel your body, which in return will also burn off body fat! That is the rule of this diet, you must eat fats! The advantage to eating dietary fats and the keto diet is that you will not feel hungry. Fat digestion is slow, which works to your advantage and helps you feel 'full'.

You will be doing this Monday - Friday and will then '' carb-up '' on the weekend. After your last workout on Friday, this is when the carb-up starts. You must intake a liquid carbohydrate along with your whey shake post workout. This helps create an insulin spike and helps get the nutrients your body desperately needs for muscle repair and growth and refill glycogen stores. During this stage (carb-up), eat what you want - pizzas, pasta, crisps, ice cream. Anything. This will be beneficial for you because it will refuel your body for the upcoming week, as well as restoring your body's nutrient needs. Once Sunday starts, it's back to the no-carb, high-fat, moderate protein diet. Keeping your body in ketosis and burning fat as energy is the perfect solution.

Another advantage to ketosis is that once your get into the state of ketosis and burn off the fat, your body will be depleted of carbs. Once you load up with carbs, you will look as full as ever (with less body fat!), which is perfect for the occasions on weekends when you go to the beach or parties!

Now let's recap on the diet.

- Must enter the state of ketosis by eliminating carbs from the diet while intaking high-fat moderate/low-protein.

- Must intake fibre of some sort to keep your pipes as clear as ever, if you know what I mean.

- Once in ketosis, protein intake must be at least that of a gram of protein per pound of lean mass.

Keto and Low-Carb Recipe Ideas: 5 Delicious Pizzas for Low-Carb and Keto Dieters

You can still eat pizza on the keto diet plan, but it takes a bit of creativity. When dining out, order a thin-crust pizza, then take your fork and slide all the toppings off the crust. It helps to order a pizza with lots of toppings. Ordering one topping on a deep dish pizza leaves you with very little left to eat.

As with most food options on keto, the best pizza is the one you make yourself. Try the low-carb pizza crust recipe, then use some of these ideas for toppings:

Mexican pizza - Use either traditional (low-carb) pizza sauce or enchilada sauce and top with taco-seasoned ground beef or chicken. Add a bit of salsa, chopped onions, chopped jalapeno peppers, and some hot sauce (Taco Bell hot sauce is the lowest in carbs). For some added flavor, add chopped cilantro. And top with sliced avocado after baking.

Greek pizza - Sauce, feta cheese, red onions, olives, and how about some artichoke hearts?

Buffalo chicken pizza - Frank's red-hot buffalo wing sauce is low in carbs. If you like hot, hot, hot, use chopped grilled chicken, some onions, crumbled blue cheese, and the buffalo sauce to make a zesty pizza. Don't forget to drizzle a little blue cheese dressing over the top.

Indian pizza - There's a local restaurant nearby that specializes in Indian pizzas,. If you choose to make this delicious option, you could use a packaged Indian food seasoning for chicken on top of the low-carb crust and add some veggies. If you want to start from scratch, season some chicken with traditional Indian spices, like masala, curry powder, cumin, and any other spicy Indian seasonings you can think of. Add veggies, if desired.

Alfredo pizza - Use a keto diet-friendly Alfredo sauce or just spoon some out of a jar. Top with chicken or shrimp, plus garlic, parsley, Roma tomatoes - and extra parmesan cheese if you'd like.

KETOGENIC DIETS FOR MANAGING TYPE 2 DIABETES

Meat lovers - Pepperoni, sausage, bacon, pork, whatever you'd like. All these are very low-carb options.

Veggie lovers - Mushrooms, onions, tomatoes, all types of peppers, artichoke hearts... you name it, it'll taste great.

Three (or four, or five) cheese pizza - Try feta cheese, blue cheese, goat cheese, cream cheese, or any other tangy cheese, in addition to -- or in place -- of the traditional shredded mozzarella (remember, many low-carb crusts are also made out of cheese. You may want to be careful with overdoing it!).

Ketogenic diets have been in use since 1924 in pediatrics as a treatment for epilepsy. A ketogenic (keto) diet is one that is high in fat and low in carbs. The design of the ketogenic diet is to shift the body's metabolic fuel from burning carbohydrates to fats. With the keto diet, the body metabolizes fat, instead of sugar, into energy. Ketones are a byproduct of that process.

Over the years, ketogenic diets have been used to treat diabetes. One justification was that it treats diabetes at its root cause by lowering carbohydrate intake leading to lower blood sugar, which in turn, reduces the need for insulin, which minimizes insulin resistance and associated metabolic syndrome. In this way, a ketogenic diet may improve blood glucose (sugar) levels, while at the same time reducing the need for insulin. This point of view presents keto diets as a much safer and more effective plan than injecting insulin to counteract the consumption of high-carbohydrate foods.

A keto diet is actually a very restrictive one. In the classic keto diet, for example, one gets about 80% of caloric requirements from fat and 20% from proteins and carbohydrates. This is a marked departure from the norm, where the body runs on energy from sugar derived from carbohydrate digestion, but by severely limiting carbohydrates, the body is forced to use fat instead.

A ketogenic diet requires a healthy food intake from beneficial fats, such as coconut oil, grass-pastured butter, organic pastured eggs, avocado, fish such as salmon, cottage cheese, avocado, almond butter, and raw nuts (raw pecans and macadamia). People on ketogenic diets avoid all bread, rice, potatoes, pasta, flour, starchy vegetables, and dairy. The diet is low in vitamins, minerals, and nutrients and requires supplementation.

A low-carbohydrate diet is frequently recommended for people with type 2 diabetes because carbohydrates turn into blood sugar, and in large quantities they cause blood sugar to spike. Thus, for a diabetic who already has high blood sugar, eating additional sugar-producing foods is like courting danger. By switching the focus from sugar to fat, some patients can experience reduced blood sugar.

Changing the body's primary energy source from carbohydrates to fat leaves behind the byproduct of fat metabolism, ketones in the blood. For some diabetic patients, this can be dangerous, as a buildup of ketones may create a risk for developing diabetic ketoacidosis (DKA). DKA is a medical emergency requiring the immediate attention of a physician. DKA signs include consistently high blood sugar, dry mouth, polyuria, nausea, breath that has a fruit-like odor, and breathing difficulties. Complications can lead to diabetic coma.

HOW TO FOLLOW A PLANT-BASED KETOGENIC DIET

So, how exactly do you slip into ketosis without loading up on butter and bacon? And how can you ensure that your nutrient needs are still being met while following a plant-based ketogenic diet?

The key is to swap out your starchy veggies for low-carb alternatives, while also filling your diet with plenty of plant-based fats and proteins. This can help you stay under your carbohydrate goal and provide your body with the important vitamins and minerals that it needs to stay healthy.

High-carb foods that should be limited in your diet include:

• High sugar fruits (apples, oranges, bananas, grapes, etc.)

• Starchy vegetables (potatoes, sweet potatoes, winter squash, peas, corn, etc.)

• Sugar (including honey, maple syrup, agave syrup,

etc.)

• Legumes (beans, lentils, peas, etc.)

• Grains (wheat products, rice, quinoa, cereal, etc.)

Instead, be sure to include plenty of nutrient-rich, low-carb, plant-based foods in your diet, such as:

• Fermented foods (tempeh, natto, etc.)

• Leafy greens (kale, chard, spinach, collard greens, etc.)

• Non-starchy vegetables (asparagus, carrots, cauliflower, onions, mushrooms, peppers, etc.)

• Nuts (almonds, walnuts, pistachios, pecans, etc.)

• Seeds (chia seeds, flax seeds, hemp seeds, pumpkin seeds, etc.)

• Low-sugar fruits (blackberries, raspberries, strawberries, etc.)

• Healthy fats (coconut oil, MCT oil, olive oil)

Including enough protein in your diet can be challenging on any plant-based diet, let alone a plant-based ketogenic diet. Fortunately, there are tons of healthy options that can provide the protein you need to keep you going.

A few examples of low-carb, plant-based proteins include:

• Tempeh

• Natto

• Nutritional Yeast

• Spirulina

• Nuts

• Seeds

•   High-quality, low-sugar plant-based protein powders

Similarly, nixing all dairy products from your diet can make it tricky to get in enough fat, but there are plenty of plant-based sources of fat available that can help you easily meet your needs.

Some of the healthiest plant-based fats include:

• Avocado Oil

• Coconut Oil

• Olive Oil

• MCT Oil

- Avocado

- Nuts

- Seeds

Note that you can easily swap these nutritious foods into your favorite recipes to make them completely plant-based and keto-friendly. Nutritional yeast, for example, makes a great substitute for cheese, while tempeh can be crumbled and cooked like ground beef to make delicious veggie tacos or lettuce wraps.

Sample Meal Plan:

Wondering what exactly a plant-based ketogenic diet looks like? Here's a one-day sample meal plan that you can follow to help get you started!

Breakfast:

Gluten-free oatmeal (2 grams net carbs per serving)

Lunch:

Baked tempeh (3 grams net carbs per serving)

Cauliflower tabbouleh salad (6 grams net carbs per serving)

Olive oil vinaigrette (0 grams net carbs per serving)

Dinner:

Raw walnut tacos (4 grams net carbs per serving)

Super cilantro guacamole (5 grams net carbs per serving)

Snacks:

Keto smoothie with avocado, chia seeds and cacao (6.5 grams net carbs)

Almonds (2.5 grams net carbs per 1-oz serving)

Spicy roasted pumpkin seeds (10 grams carbs per 1-oz serving)

Daily Total: 39 grams net carbs

CHAPTER SIX

WHAT A VEGAN CAN EAT ON THEIR KETO JOURNEY

But can a vegetarian or vegan be keto? Does the necessity of fat and the small margin for carbs eliminate anyone else for meat and dairy consumers? No. Vegetarians and vegans can still be LCHF while observing their food preferences. Here at Keys to Ketosis, we've provided a vegan ketogenic diet food list to help anyone who is conscious of what types of food they consume, but still wants to (or has to) pursue a low-carb, high-fat lifestyle.

Check out the list of compiled low-carb vegan diet foods below

Tofu

The point of tension for a vegan/vegetarian attempting to pursue a LCHF will be the choices for a base food or "main course" food that will provide much of their protein and fat sources.

On the vegan ketogenic diet food list, Tofu will be one of the big operators for finding interesting ways to create mindful foods that also assist you in your low-carb pursuit. Tofu is a versatile food, that comes in various forms and can be cooked in a variety of ways, including grilling, frying, baking, or just eating it raw. Having this on your vegan ketogenic diet food list will be imperative to maintaining excitement and variety.

Tofu Nutriton Facts (1/2 Cup):

Calories: 94

Fats: 6g

Carbs: 2.3g

Protein: 10g

Nuts

Nuts are a must on the ketogenic diet, but peanuts should be eaten judiciously, due to their classification of legume, which means they belong to the same family as beans, and share their high-carb profiles. However, you can use peanut butter for a topping, but once again, not in excess.

The good news for your vegan ketogenic diet food list is that there are plenty of nuts that are permissible – and beneficial – due to being low-carb high-fat.

The best of the best include the following (in descending order from best to worst):

• Almonds

• Macadamia Nuts

• Walnuts

• Pecans

• Cashews and Pistachios

Nut-based flours can also be used for baking instead of high-carb wheat flour.

MCT Oil

MCT oil will make staying LCHF on a vegan diet easier than it has ever been.

MCT oil for the keto diet plan

By using this supplement in shakes, as a dressing, or on other foods, you can ensure that your body is getting the correct doses of fatty acids that are essential to ketosis.

Other ideas:

Mixing in toppings (like mayo)

Use while baking food instead of regular baking oil

The great thing about using MCT oil (and other exogenous ketones) is that you can counterbalance some of the carbs you will inevitably take by adhering to the vegan ketogenic diet food list.

Olive and Coconut Oil

Other oils that are great for toppings or cooking are coconut and olive oil. Both of these oils provide a great source of healthy fats, and a broad range of uses for food.

Olive oil in the vegan ketogenic diet food list

And unlike MCT oil, these oils can be used for frying and sautéing food. Coconut oil is more stable than olive oil, so it is the better choice for using at high temperatures.

Vegan ketogenic diet food list uses coconut oil

The benefit that these two oils bring to your vegan ketogenic diet food list, is their ability to provide vibrancy with flavor. While MCT oil can provide a more potent shot of healthy fat, it can also bring with it a taste that can be hard to handle if not masked, whereas coconut and olive oil are both pleasurable to consume.

Greens

Since fruits are a no on the ketogenic diet (except for avocados), you will need to be strategic about eating enough greens to get the nutrients you'd obtain from the fruits you'd normally consume on a standard vegan diet.

Leafy greens on the vegan ketogenic diet food list

The vegetables that you should keep stocked on your ketogenic diet food list are leafy greens like kale, collard greens, spinach, swiss chard, and others of the same family.

These vegetables, mixed with avocados and keto-friendly oils (listed above) will help you stay vibrant from proper vitamin intake, while also helping you maintain a low-carb lifestyle.

Fatty Produce (Avocado)

The avocado is the hallmark of healthy fats from fruits (yes, avocados are a fruit). It is also capable of being used in every meal of the day, pairing well with salads. Did we mention that guacamole is incredible?

Avocado in the vegan ketogenic diet food list

Avocados are considered a superfood, because research suggests they help lower cholesterol, and even ward off cancer!

Nutrition Info (1 avocado):

Calories: 322

Fats: 29g

Carbs: 17g

Protein: 4g

SOME MYTHS ON LOW-CARB DIETS

MYTH: Low carb diets are bad for health

Although pretty much all dietitians agree that cutting out sugar and refined flour is a good idea, there is still no consensus about low-carb nutrition amongst professionals. There are many scientific studies that show low-carb dieting to be not only not dangerous, but actually good for your health in many ways beyond weight loss. Specifically, it has been found that following some low-carb diet plans can improve digestion and levels of cholesterol.

Quite often, dietitians who don't specialise in low-carb nutrition (and so don't necessarily know much about it) have a knee-jerk negative reaction when asked about low-carb diets. For example, they often cite possible lack of vitamins as a negative factor. This is simply not true. Most low-carb diets do allow plenty of vegetables, and in fact, some people find that low-carb dieting means they start eating more vegetables, since that's their only permitted source of carbs.

However, as is the case with nutrition in general - whether trying to lose weight or not - it is important to be sensible and follow a plan that's been developed and tested by experts. If you suddenly stop eating all carbs and try to live on steak, cheese, and bacon, then clearly that would not be good for you. Contrary to the negative stereotype, this is not at all what low-carb dieting is all about. Choose a low-carb diet to suit your lifestyle, and then get the book and read it, so that you know exactly how to devise and manage your diet plan.

MYTH: Ketosis is dangerous

Being in ketosis means that fat is processed for energy instead of carbohydrates. Millions of people have experienced this state without any adverse health effects. Ketogenic diets are prescribed by mainstream medical professionals for managing symptoms of some diseases such as epilepsy.

Ketosis is sometimes confused with ketoacidosis, which is indeed a dangerous state but it only affects people with type 1 diabetes.

MYTH: Low-carb is not a natural way to eat

In fact, what's really unnatural is the standard Western diet that is high in refined sugar and flour. Typical high-carb foods that are so abundant today are a result of technological advancement, and have only been available for the last century or two. There is nothing natural about white sugar - it is a result of a complicated refining process.

Going even further back, humans as a species have been hunters and fishers since long before they learned how to cultivate grains and other plant-based foods. Whatever plants or roots were available in those primitive societies, would have contained a lot less carbs than their modern-day counterparts, as they have by now been cultivated and bred selectively for centuries.

Finally, bear in mind that our lifestyles in the modern day are very different to those of our ancestors, even going back as early as a century ago. Technological progress means that most of us lead sedentary lives and do very little physical work. In developed countries, food is abundant and no one ever starves (sadly, this is not the case in some other areas of the world). Technology develops much too fast for a human body to evolve accordingly. Perhaps one day humans will evolve out of their basic need to consume and store food whenever they can. But in our lifetime, we will have to stick with diet and exercise to mitigate the consequences of food abundance.

MYTH: Low-carb dieters never get to eat any fruit or vegetables, and so may lack in vitamins

The myth about no fruit or vegetables is probably the most persistent one out there, and again, it is just simply not true. Most low-carb diets allow plenty of vegetables, and fruit is only restricted during the early phases of some plans.

Whilst there is no debate about vegetables, the way we think about fruit is actually sometimes misguided. We have come to think of them automatically as healthy, but in reality, some fruit are extremely high in sugar. Eating several oranges or a pack of grapes in one go gives you the same amount of sugar as a chocolate bar would. Whilst of course fruit would be better than chocolate (as it also contains fibre and vitamins), sugar is still sugar, and you should eat less of it if you want to lose weight. Fruit juices remove fibre from the fruit, and in fact are hardly better than sugary fizzy drinks.

If you are worried about getting enough vitamins in the early, more restrictive stages of your diet, consider taking a multivitamin supplement.

MYTH: Not getting enough carbs will make me tired

It is true that you may experience a short period of tiredness while your body adjusts. However, this period usually only lasts for several days. Once your body switches to burning fat instead of carbohydrates for energy, you are likely to find yourself feeling more energetic than before. Moreover, you will feel so on a consistent and continuous basis - in contrast to roller-coaster up and down energy levels typical of a high-carb diet.

CHAPTER SEVEN

INFLAMMATION - EATING ANTI-INFLAMMATORY FOODS

Are there really diets out there that can reduce inflammation? Do they work? Scientists have found that there is a relationship, in part, between what we eat and inflammation. They've even identified some compounds in food that can reduce inflammation and others that promote it. There is still a lot to learn about just how diet and inflammation interact, and research, as of yet, is not at that point where a specific foods or groups of foods can be singled out as being beneficial for people with, for example, arthritis. We are beginning to get a clearer picture of how eating the right way can reduce inflammation.

So why are we so concerned about inflammation? Inflammation is the body's natural defense to infections and injuries. When something goes wrong, the body's immune system goes to work to inflame the area, which serves to get rid of the invader or to heal the wound. Inflammation can cause pain, swelling, redness, and warmth, but this goes away as soon as the problem is solved. This is good inflammation.

Then we have chronic inflammation, the type that's familiar to people with rheumatoid arthritis (RA), lupus, psoriatic arthritis, and other types of "inflammatory" arthritis. Chronic inflammation is the type that will not go away. All the types of arthritis that are mentioned above are a disorder of the immune system which creates inflammation and then doesn't know when to shut off. Inflammatory arthritis' chronic inflammation can have serious consequences, permanent disability and tissue damage can be done if it isn't treated properly. Inflammation has been linked to a full host of other medical conditions.

Inflammation has been found to contribute to atherosclerosis, which is when fat builds up on the lining of arteries, raising the risk of heart attacks. Also, high levels of inflammation proteins have been found in the blood of people with heart disease. Inflammation has also been linked to obesity, diabetes, asthma, depression, and even Alzheimer's disease and cancer. Scientists think that a constant level of inflammation in the body, even if the level is low, can have a number of negative effects. Research shows that a diet can reduce inflammation; in theory an inflammation-lowering diet should have an effect on a wide range of health conditions.

Researchers have looked for clues in the eating habits of our early ancestors to discover which foods might benefit us the most. They believe those habits are more in tune to our eating habits with how the body processes and uses what we eat and drink. Our ancestors' diet consisted of wild lean meats (venison or boar) and wild plants (green leafy vegetables, fruits, nuts, and berries). There were no cereal grains until the agriculture revolution (about 10,000 years ago). There was very little dairy, and there were no processed or refined foods. Our diets are usually are high in meat, saturated (or bad) fats, and processed foods, and there is very little exercise. Nearly everything we eat is available close by or as far away as our computer and the click of a mouse.

Our diet and lifestyles are way out of whack with how our bodies are made from the inside out. While our genetic make-up has changed very little from our early beginnings, our diet and lifestyles have changed a great deal, and the changes have gotten worse over the last 50 to 100 years. Our genes haven't had a chance to adapt. We aren't giving our bodies the right kind of fuel, it's as though we think of our bodies as engines in a jet plane, when instead they are like the engine in the very first planes. There are some foods that we are putting into our bodies, especially because we are eating way too much of them, that are affecting our health in a bad way.

There are two nutrients in our diets that have attracted attention, which are omega-3 fatty acids and omega-6 fatty acids that have been part of our diets for thousands of years. They are components in just about all of our many cells and are important for normal growth and development. Both of these acids play a role in inflammation. In several studies it was found that certain sources of omega-3s in particular, help to reduce the inflammation process and that omega-6s will raise it.

Now this is the problem, the average American eats on average about 15 times more omega-6s than omega-3s. While our very early ancestor's ate omega-6s and omega-3s in equal ratio, and it is believed that this is what helped to balance their ability to turn inflammation on and off. The imbalance of omega-3s and omega-6s in our diets is believed to contribute to the excess of inflammation in our bodies.

So why is it that we eat so many omega-6s now? Vegetable oils such as corn oil, safflower oil, sunflower oil, cottonseed oil, soybean oil, and the products made from them, such as margarine, are loaded with omega-6s. Even many of the processed snack foods that are so readily available today are full of these oils. Based on the best information of the time, the best suggestion was to use vegetable oils like those mentioned above instead of foods with saturated fats such as butter and lard. It looks like the consequences of that advice may have contributed to the increased consumption of omega-6s and therefore caused an imbalance of omega-3s and omega-6s.

You can find omega-6s in other common foods such as meats and egg yolks. The omega-6 found in meat is the fatty acids that come from grain-fed animals such as cows, lambs, pigs, and chickens. Most of the meat sold in America is grain-fed, unlike their grass-fed cousins who contain less of those fatty acids. Wild game such as venison and boar are lower in omega-6s and fat and higher in omega-3s than the meat that comes from the supermarkets where we shop.

You can get omega-3s in both animal and plant foods. Our bodies can convert omega-3s from animal sources into anti-inflammatory compounds more easily than the omega-3s from plant sources. Plant foods contain hundreds of other healthful compounds, many of which are anti-inflammatory, so don't discount them all together.

There are many foods that are high in omega-3s and those include fatty fish, especially fish from cold waters. Of course everyone knows about salmon, but did you know that you can also find omega-3s in mackerel, anchovies, sardines, herring, striped bass, and bluefish? It's also widely known that wild fish are better sources of omega-3s than farm-raised ones. You can also buy eggs that have been enriched with omega-3 oils. There are several excellent sources of omega-3s in plants that are leafy greens (like kale, Swiss chard, and spinach) as well as flaxseed, wheat germ, walnuts, and their oils.

You can also get omega-3s in supplements (often as fish oil); this source has been shown to be beneficial in some instances. You should talk with your doctor before you take a fish oil supplement because it can interact with some medications and under certain circumstances can increase the risk of bleeding. I take a prescribed omega-3 supplement because my doctor had told me that the ones you get in the supermarket or health food store are not pure, they have other additives that do absolutely nothing to help. There are other fats that are contributors to clogged arteries, the "bad" or saturated fats found in meats and high-fat dairy foods, which are called pro-inflammatory.

There are also the trans fats that are relatively new to the cause of heart disease. These trans fats can be found in processed convenience and snack foods and can be spotted by reading the labels. They can be identified as partially hydrogenated oils, often soybean oil or cottonseed oil. But, they can also occur naturally in small amounts in animal foods. The thought is that they contribute to the pro-inflammatory activities in our bodies and the amounts we eat today are staggering.

Antioxidants are substances that prevent inflammation, causing "free radicals" to overtake our bodies. Plant foods such as fruits, vegetables (including beans), nuts, and seeds carry high amounts of antioxidants. Extra-virgin olive oil and walnut oil are very good sources of antioxidants, as well. These foods have long been considered the basics for good health, and can be found in fruits and vegetables with colorful and vibrant pigments. The more colorful the plant, the better they are for you, from green vegetables, especially leafy ones, to low-starch vegetables, such as broccoli and cauliflower, to berries, tomatoes, and brightly-colored orange and yellow fruits and vegetables.

We don't have to revert back completely to the caveman to eat the anti-inflammatory way to benefit from the anti-inflammatory diet. Just eating a healthful diet that is recommended today is right on track. Our chief strategy should be to balance the amount of modern-day foods with those of long ago, which were rich in the inflammation reducing foods. Really, all we have to do is replace foods rich in omega-6 with foods rich in omega-3, cutting down on how much meat and poultry we eat while eating oily fish a couple of times a week and adding more varieties of colorful fruits and vegetables, and while whole grains were not a part of our early ancestor's diet, they should be included in ours. Be sure that it is whole grains and not refined grains because they contain many beneficial nutrients and inflammation-tempering compounds. Researchers have found that eating a lot of foods high in sugar and white flour may promote inflammation, although there is more studying that needs to be done on the subject.

The amounts of knowledge we have on how the body works and how our ancestors ate is helping to confirm the old adage: "You are what you eat." But, there is still more we need to learn before we can prescribe any one anti-inflammatory diet. Our genetic makeup and the severity of our health condition will determine the benefits we get from an anti-inflammatory diet and unfortunately there is doubt that there will be one regimen that fits us all.

Also, what we eat or don't eat is just a small part of the whole story. We are not as physically active as our ancestors and exercise has its own anti-inflammatory effects. Our ancestors were also much leaner than we are and body fat is active tissue that can make inflammatory producing compounds.

Anti-inflammatory eating is a way of selecting foods that are more in tune with what the body actually needs. We can achieve a more balanced diet by going back to our roots. If you look at the diet of the people of the Bible, you will find that they, like our caveman ancestors, were more active and their diets consisted of much the same things as our caveman ancestors. They also had no choice but to walk everywhere they wanted to go, there was no such thing as cars or trucks. While we have it easier today, our health has suffered greatly from it.

CHAPTER EIGHT

KETOGENIC DIET FREQUENTLY ASKED QUESTIONS

Here are some answers to some of the most commonly asked questions...

Why do I keep reverting back to my old "out of shape" self?

You work out for a few months and get in shape and fall back to the old habits because you were not conditioned mentally, only physically. Physical fitness is only a part of journey, and fitness is over 75% percent mental. Gyms, nutritionists, and personal trainers give most people a temporary Band-Aid but never address the actual issue.

How do you know when your body is in ketosis?

Any of these signs may indicate you are in ketosis:

Decreased appetite and increased energy levels.

Increased thirst and urination.

"Keto breath", which may be more apparent to others than to yourself

Dry mouth or a metallic taste in your mouth.

Beyond these signs and symptoms, you can measure your level of ketosis, using one of three methods:

1. Urine strips

2. Breath analyzers

3. Blood meters

What foods can you eat on a keto diet?

Eat real low-carb foods like meat, fish, eggs, vegetables, and natural fats (like olive oil or butter). A simple rule for beginners is to eat foods with fewer than 5% carbs

Is a keto diet safe for the kidneys?

Yes. People often wonder about this, because of the belief that a diet high in protein could be harmful for the kidneys. However, this fear is simply based on two misunderstandings:

A keto diet is high in fat, not protein.

People with normal kidney function handle excessive protein just fine.

Is ketosis safe for diabetics?

A keto diet leading to ketosis is generally a very powerful treatment to reverse type 2 diabetes.

People with type 1 diabetes can use a keto or low-carb diet to significantly improve their blood-sugar control. They will however normally always require insulin injections, but usually far lower doses on keto. They need to take care to not take too low doses and end up with ketoacidosis, or too high and end up with keto.

Both people with type 1 and type 2 may rapidly require a reduction in medication on a keto diet to avoid hypoglycemia.

How many carbs can you eat and still be in ketosis?

This varies, but generally it's a good idea to stay below 20 net carbs per day.

Some people who are not insulin-resistant – e.g. lean, young people who exercise regularly – can sometimes tolerate more carbs, perhaps 50 grams or more per day.

Is a ketogenic diet safe for high cholesterol?

Generally, the cholesterol profile tends to improve on a keto diet, lowering triglycerides and raising the good HDL cholesterol.

However, a small minority of people may end up with quite high total cholesterol. Whether this is dangerous or safe is debated – there are no quality studies to determine the answer. But should you be one of the few where cholesterol may get up very high, e.g. over 400, you may want to take steps to reduce it just to be safe.

Can I have fruit on a keto diet?

Although fruits are often considered healthy, they are actually very high in carbs and sugar, unlike non-starchy vegetables. Therefore, when it comes to keto diets, most fruits should be avoided.

However, certain berries are an exception that can be enjoyed in small amounts. The best choices are blackberries, raspberries, and strawberries, which provide 5-6 grams of carbs per 100 grams (3½ ounces).

Most other fruits – including blueberries – contain double or triple this amount of carbs, as reflected in this guide to the best and worst fruits in terms of carb content.

Keep in mind that berries don't provide any nutrients that can't be found in vegetables and other foods with fewer carbs, so they are entirely optional on a keto diet. In fact, if you are very insulin-resistant, you might be better off not having them.

How long can someone be on a keto diet?

As long as you want to, and enjoy it.

Can I eat a keto diet as a vegetarian or vegan?

A keto diet can work for many non-meat-eaters, depending on what other types of food their diets include.

A lacto-ovo vegetarian eats dairy and eggs, whereas a lacto-vegetarian eats dairy but doesn't eat eggs. There is also a subset of vegetarians known as pescatarians who include fish in their diet but avoid poultry and other meat.

Although following keto as a vegetarian is definitely doable, it can be a little challenging, especially when first starting out.

A keto vegetarian meal plan provides several well-balanced, healthy meat-free meals.

On the other hand, a ketogenic vegan diet isn't a well-balanced or sustainable option. Because vegans exclude all animal products, they must rely on a combination of grains, legumes, and seeds to get all the essential amino acids their bodies need. For this reason, a keto diet and vegan diet don't work well together. Therefore, you'll need to make a choice between the two or consider following a keto vegetarian diet.

What should my ketone level be in ketosis?

Generally above 0.5 mmol/l.

What can I do for keto breath?

How to handle keto breath.

Can I have dairy on keto?

Dairy is nutritious and can be part of a keto diet in many cases. However, whether you personally should eat dairy may depend on your health goals, along with your personal response to it.

For instance, although a higher dairy intake has been linked to fat loss and reduced diabetes risk in several studies, it has also been found to raise insulin levels. Indeed, some people find that cutting back on dairy helps with weight loss.

It's also important to avoid high-carb options typically considered "healthy," such as nonfat milk and nonfat yogurt. Instead, focus on these high-fat choices, preferably from naturally raised animals:

- Butter

- Cream

- Sour cream

- Cream cheese

- Cheese

- Plain whole-milk yogurt, Greek yogurt, or kefir

Can you build muscle on keto?

Yes.

What's the difference between low-carb and keto diets?

Keto is a very strict low-carb diet, that also puts even more emphasis on moderating the protein intake, and relying primarily on fat to supply energy needs.

A regular strict low-carb diet will likely put most people in ketosis anyway. But a keto diet tweaks things even further to make sure it's working and, if desired, to get even deeper into ketosis.

Keto could be called an extra strict low-carb diet.

Why am I not in ketosis?

The two most common reasons for not getting into ketosis are:

Too many carbs

Too much protein

Should you aim for high ketone levels to speed up weight loss?

Yes and no. Eating fewer carbs, less protein, and doing intermittent fasting certainly promotes weight loss, while lowering insulin and raising ketones.

However, adding extra fat to raise ketone levels does not promote weight loss. Neither does supplementing with MCT oil to raise ketone levels, or drinking "exogenous" ketone supplements. These methods actually slow down weight loss, by providing alternative fuel to be used instead of burning body fat.

If you want to lose weight, only use these methods – MCT oil or exogenous ketones – when you are hungry, or for performance reasons (unrelated to weight loss).

At what time of the day should you test ketone levels?

For comparison purposes, it's good to measure about

the same time every day. Measuring in the morning before eating makes it easier to compare the result from day to day.

However, morning numbers are usually among the lowest of the day, while evening numbers are higher. So if for some reason you want impressively high numbers, measure in the evenings instead. Be aware that your ketone levels don't distinguish between the burning of dietary fat and stored fat.

Is keto safe during pregnancy?

A keto diet appears to be safe during pregnancy, judging from the experiences of people who have done it and doctors used to treating patients using a keto diet during pregnancy. It may also be very helpful in cases of gestational diabetes.

However, there are no scientific studies on the subject, so there is a lack of definite knowledge. Possibly it's wise to exercise caution and aim for a more moderate low-carb diet during pregnancy, unless there are important health benefits of doing a keto diet in your specific case.

How To Know If You're In Ketosis

You can measure if you're in ketosis via urine or blood strips, although it is pretty simple to just use physical indicators to tell if you are "spilling ketones."

Here is a list of "symptoms" that usually let you know if you're in a state of ketosis:

Increased Urination. Ketones act as a natural diuretic, so you have to go to the bathroom more. Acetoacetate, a ketone body, is also excreted in urination and can lead to increased bathroom visits for beginners.

Dry Mouth. The increased urination leads to dry mouth and increased thirst. Make sure that you're drinking plenty of water and replenishing your electrolytes (salt, potassium, magnesium).

Bad Breath. Acetone is a ketone body that partially excretes in our breath. It can smell sharp like overripe fruit, similar to nail polish remover. It's usually temporary and goes away after a short while.

Reduced Hunger and Increased Energy. After you get past the initial stages of the ketogenic diet and your body had adjusted, you'll experience a much lower hunger level and a "clear" or energized mental state.

Note: Many people end up driving themselves crazy measuring and testing! It's much better to focus on the nutritional aspect, making sure that you're consuming proper foods and staying within your macro ranges.

The Ketogenic Diet: Bottom Line

The Ketogenic Diet: Not only does the ketogenic diet help you to lose weight and alter your metabolic state, but it will also help you to become healthier overall by lowering your cholesterol and blood pressure, regulating your insulin levels, giving you more energy, eliminating unhealthy food cravings, and improving your mental performance.

Admittedly, the keto diet can be intimidating at first, but it is a truly empowering way of life once you grasp the concept and start seeing the results!

When you limit your carbohydrate intake you will primarily get your 15g of carbs or more a day from nuts, dairy, and vegetables. You will be encouraged to AVOID potatoes, beans, fruit, legumes, bread, pasta, cereal, and any sugar (refined carbs and starches).

There are a few exceptions to these foods once you have maintained ketosis for a while, such as berries and star fruit, and avocado can be consumed later in the diet in moderation.

Here are a few examples of the "do eat" and "do not eat" foods list for the keto diet:

Do Not Eat

1. Grains – wheat, corn, rice, cereal, etc.

2. Sugar – honey, agave, maple syrup, etc.

3. Fruit – apples, bananas, oranges, etc.

4. Tubers – potato, yams, etc.

Do Eat

1. Meats – fish, beef, lamb, poultry, eggs, etc.

2. Leafy Greens – spinach, kale, etc.

3. Above ground vegetables – broccoli, cauliflower, etc.

4. High Fat Dairy – hard cheeses, high fat cream, butter, etc.

5. Nuts and seeds – macadamias, walnuts, sunflower seeds, etc.

6. Avocado and berries – raspberries, blackberries, and other low glycemic impact berries, etc.

7. Sweeteners – stevia, erythritol, monk fruit, etc.

Ingredients:

2 cups cheese of your choice (use a Parmesan-Romano mix along with some Swiss and cheddar)

1 cup almond flour

2 oz cream cheese

1 egg

1/2 teaspoon sea salt

1 teaspoon rosemary (or a seasoning of your choice such as basil, chives, garlic, dill weed, spicy chili, thyme, oregano etc...)

Instructions:

Mix all the cheeses (including the cream cheese) along with the almond flour in a microwave safe bowl and cook it for exactly one minute(there are some people that prefer not to use a microwave and I certainly understand that. You can heat these ingredients up on the stove top too. You are going to heat them up just enough for the cheese to my melted enough for you to roll out the dough. I would continue stirring it while heating it up on the stove top).

Immediately stir the ingredients until the almond flour and cheeses have combined fully. You want the cheese to be partially melted.

Allow this to cool for a few minutes because if you put the egg in these ingredients too soon it will cook the egg.

Now add the egg, sea salt, and seasoning of your choice. I decided to cut up some fresh rosemary I had on hand. You want to add about a teaspoon of your favorite seasoning unless it's a spicy mix. I would add only about a 1/2 teaspoon for spicy seasonings.

Mix it together until all the ingredients are fully combined. If you cheese has gotten too hard or it's too hard to mix, you can microwave your cheese for another 20 seconds to get it soft again.

Now you will place the ball of dough on a large sheet of parchment paper. Then place another sheet of parchment paper of equal size on top of the ball of dough.

You can use your hands or a rolling pin to spread the dough out into a thin layer. It spread so easily that I used my hands to have more control and keep the dough inside the square piece of parchment paper. Make sure the parchment paper is the same size as your baking sheet.

Next, use a pizza cutter to cut the crackers into small squares as seen in the photos.

Bake these crackers on each side at 450 degrees for about 5 or 6 minutes on each side. If the crackers are thin, you will cook them about 5 minutes on each side but if the dough is thick, it may take 7 to 9 minutes to get the crispy cracker texture you are looking for. When you keep the dough on the parchment paper it's really easy to flip it over while it's hot after cooking it on the first side.- Feel free to leave the crackers in the oven longer (but watch them closely) if you love a very crispy texture. The crispier the better for me!

Allow the crackers to cool for about 5 minutes and they are ready to eat!

INGREDIENTS FOR KETO PRETZELS:

Ingredients:

3 cups Mozzarella cheese, shredded

4 tablespoons of cream cheese

1 ½ cups of almond flour

2 teaspoons of xanthum gum

2 Eggs, at room temperature

2 teaspoons of dried yeast, approximately 1 sachet

2 tablespoons of warm water

2 tablespoons of butter, melted

1 tablespoon of pretzel salt

How To Make Keto Soft Pretzels:

Preheat oven to 200C/390F.

In a microwave safe dish, place the mozzarella cheese and cream cheese and microwave in 30 sec increments, stirring in between, until fully melted and almost liquid.

Dissolve the yeast in the warm water and allow it to sit and activate for 2 minutes.

In your stand mixer (using the dough hook attachment), place the almond meal and xanthum gum and mix well.

Add the eggs, yeast mixture and 1 tablespoon of the melted butter and mix well.

Add the hot melted cheese to the stand mixer and allow it to knead the dough until all the ingredients are fully combined. Around 5-10 minutes.

Split the dough into 12 balls. The dough is easiest to work with while it is warm.

Roll each ball into a long skinny log and twist into a pretzel shape. Place on a lined cookie sheet and give a little space with side as the pretzels will rise.

Brush the pretzels with the remaining butter and sprinkle with pretzel salt.

Bake in the oven for 12-15 minutes.

When the pretzels are golden brown, remove them from the oven. Don't burn your fingers trying to eat them immediately.

If you're looking for a sweet version of these keto pretzels try our glazed pretzels. Our glazed pretzels taste like a low-carb doughnut.

PALEO BROWNIES RECIPE

TOTAL TIME - 40 minutes

Ingredients:

½ cup coconut oil

2 eggs

⅓ cup dark chocolate chips

½–¾ cup maple sugar

¾ teaspoon Himalayan pink salt

3 tablespoons arrowroot starch

¼-½ cup cocoa or cacao powder

2 teaspoons vanilla

Instructions:

Preheat oven to 350 F.

Melt the coconut oil and chocolate chips in a small

pot over medium heat.

Using a hand mixer, mix all the other ingredients together until the batter is thick.

Pour contents into an 8.5" X 4.5" X 2.75" loaf pan.

Bake for 30 minutes.

Allow to cool for 15 minutes.

Do you know what else? This Paleo brownie recipe is no harder or more time-consuming than a traditional brownie recipe. Plus, you loose nothing in the flavor department. This recipe includes dark chocolate chips, Himalayan pink salt, vanilla extract, coconut oil... Before you start making your delicious Paleo brownies, you'll need to preheat your oven to 350 F.

Next, in a small pot, after melting the coconut oil, add chocolate chips over medium heat.

Now you can start combining all of your other ingredients into a large mixing bowl, starting with sea salt and maple sugar...

Add the arrowroot starch...

- Stir in the vanilla extract.

Using a hand mixer, mix all the other ingredients together until the batter is thick.

Bake for 30 minutes.

I know it's hard to wait, but allow these delicious brownies to cool for 15 minutes before digging your teeth into one

STUFFED MUSHROOMS RECIPE

TOTAL TIME - 25 minutes

Ingredients:

1 tablespoon melted coconut oil, divided

20 cremini mushroom caps

1 package uncured turkey bacon

1 head of cauliflower, chopped

¼ cup grated raw goat cheese

½ teaspoon minced garlic

1 tablespoon sea salt

1 tablespoon pepper

2 tablespoons unsalted grass-fed butter, diced into 20 pieces

½ cup chives

Instructions:

Heat the oven to 400 F.

Brush the mushroom caps with the coconut oil and place them top down on a baking sheet.

Use the remaining oil to grease another baking sheet.

Distribute the bacon evenly on the greased baking sheet.

Bake the mushrooms and bacon for 15 minutes.

While the mushrooms and bacon are baking, bring a medium pot of water to a boil.

Add the cauliflower and boil for 8 minutes, or until tender.

Drain the cauliflower well and remove any excess water by patting with paper towels.

Do not allow the cauliflower to cool.

To the bowl of a food processor, add the cauliflower, cheese, garlic, salt and pepper and puree until almost smooth.

Set aside.

Remove the mushrooms and bacon from the oven.

Chop up the bacon.

Flip the mushroom caps and fill them with the cauliflower mixture.

Place one piece of butter on top of the mixture.

Crumble and sprinkle the bacon on top of each mushroom.

Serve immediately.

KETO BANANA WALNUT BREAD RECEPIE:

Ingredients:

3 Medium Bananas

2 Cups Almond Flour

3 Large Eggs

1/2 Cup Walnuts

1/4 Cup Olive Oil

1 Tsp Baking Soda

Coconut Oil

Instructions:

Preheat oven to 350

Grease loaf pan using coconut oil

Cut up bananas

Add all ingredients in a mixing bowl and mix on high until well combined

Pour mix into loaf pan and bake for 50-60 minutes

Keto Banana Walnut Bread Recipe: Nutrition

This is for one serving (makes 10 servings)

PORRIDGE

Textured vegetable protein (dry soy granules) are usually used in savory recipes, but it actually has a neutral flavor which means they can also be used in sweet recipes! If you cook them with soy or almond milk, sweetener and some cinnamon, they actually taste quite similar to oatmeal, making a nice high protein low carb breakfast porridge

This recipe makes a single serving, but you can easily double or triple it etc. to make more. If you let the porridge cool down it will keep for a few days in the fridge. You can heat up a portion when you are hungry or even just eat it cold.

Ingredients:

1/3 cup tvp granules

2/3 cup unsweetened plant milk (for instance soy or almond)

1/4 teaspoon cinnamon

low carb sweetener to taste

optional: vanilla extract, nutmeg, fruit etc.

Instructions:

Put all the ingredients into a small pot and bring it to a boil. Turn down the heat and let it cook for 10-15 minutes, until the tvp is soft. Stir often so the porridge won't burn to the bottom of the pot. Eat it warm or let it cool down and eat it cold. It will keep for a few days in the fridge

GRANOLA WITH ALPRO SOY

Time: preparation 5 minutes,

Cooking 10 minutes

Total 15 minutes

Ingredients:

1 cup sunflower seeds

1/2 cup pumpkin seeds

1/2 cup shredded dried coconut

concentrated liquid sweetener to taste (optional)

1/4 cup whole flax seed

1/4 cup ground flax seed

Instructions:

Preheat a skillet to medium high on your stove. Pour in the sunflower and pumpkin seeds and toast them until they start to turn golden brown. Stir well while toasting, so they don't burn.

Take the pan off the heat and and the shredded coconut. Stir in the sweetener until the granola is sweet enough for your taste.

Sprinkle in the whole and ground flax (don't do this earlier, or the flax will absorb the liquid sweetener, making it difficult to distribute it evenly over the granola).

Let the granola cool completely and transfer it to an airtight container. It will keep for at least a month in your pantry, and much longer in the fridge or freezer.

THAI PEANUT-PINEAPPLE FRIED RICE

Prep Time 15min.

Total Time 35min.

Put sweet and savory deliciousness on the menu with Thai Peanut-Pineapple Fried Rice. Thai Peanut-Pineapple Fried Rice is ready to eat in 35 minutes.

Ingredients:

1/4 cup teriyaki sauce

8 oz. firm tofu, cubed

1 Tbsp. PLANTERS Peanut Oil

1 red pepper, cut into strips

1/2 cup green onion pieces (1 inch)

2-2/3 cups cooked long-grain brown rice, chilled

1 can (8 oz.) pineapple tidbits in juice, drained

1/2 cup PLANTERS COCKTAIL Peanuts, chopped

Instructions:

Pour teriyaki sauce over tofu in shallow dish. Refrigerate 10 min. Drain tofu, reserving the teriyaki sauce.

Heat oil in large skillet on medium heat. Add tofu; cook 3 to 4 min. or until golden brown on all sides, stirring occasionally. Remove tofu from skillet.

Add peppers to skillet; cook and stir 2 min. Add onions; cook and stir 1 min. Add rice and pineapple; mix lightly. Cook 2 to 3 min. or until heated through, stirring frequently. Add nuts, tofu and reserved teriyaki sauce; mix lightly. Cook 2 to 3 min. or until heated through, stirring occasionally.

KETO EGG MUFFINS RECIPE

Ingredients:

6 eggs

1 scallion

5 oz. cooked bacon

3 oz. shredded cheese

1 tablespoon of red or green pesto

salt and pepper

Instructions:

Preheat the oven to 350 degrees F. and place muffin cups in baking pan. Chop the scallions and bacon and in a bowl whisk eggs with pesto and seasoning. Add cheese. Scoop batter into muffing cups and add bacon. Bake muffins for 15-20 minutes.

TURKEY OR BEEF CHILI

Ingredients:

2 pounds of ground beef or turkey

8 cups spinach

1 cup tomato sauce

2 medium green peppers

2/3 medium onion

1 tablespoon olive oil

1 tablespoon cumin

1.5 tablespoons chili powder

2 teaspoons cayenne pepper

1 teaspoon garlic powder

salt and pepper

Instructions:

Chop the onion and bell pepper. Add olive oil to a pot and cook beef or turkey until browned. While meat is cooking, saute vegetable in a separate pan with olive oil. Season both the meat and veggies with salt and pepper. Add cumin, chili powder, garlic powder, and cayenne pepper to meat. Once the meat is cooked, add spinach and let it cook for 2-3 minutes. Add tomato sauce to the pot and cook for 10 minutes. Add cooked vegetables and stir well.

CAULIFLOWER-CRUST PIZZA

Ingredients:

2 cups cauliflower rice

2 tablespoons coconut oil

1 teaspoon dried oregano

1 teaspoon garlic powder

1 large egg white

1 cup shredded mozzarella cheese

3/4 cup grated parmesan cheese

1/2 teaspoon salt

1/4 cup marinara

1/2 cup grated mozzarella cheese (for topping)

3 oz. pepperoni slices (optional)

1-2 tablespoons basil leaves (garnish)

1 tablespoon olive oil (garnish)

Instructions:

Preheat oven to 400 degrees F. Grate parmesan and mozzarella cheese into a bowl. Keep some cheese on the side for topping. Heat a large pan with coconut oil and add cauli-rice. Season with salt and cook for 15 minutes. Remove from heat and place cauli-rice into a bowl. Add 1 cup of mozzarella and 3/4 cup of parmesan cheese to rice. Also add garlic powder, dried oregano, and one egg white. Combine and mix well with hands. Flatten this dough onto parchment paper on a pizza tray and brush on coconut oil. Bake dough in oven for 15-20 minutes before flipping it over to cook the other side for 10 additional minutes. When the dough is cooked, spread marinara sauce on top and add remaining mozzarella and parmesan cheese on top. Top with pepperoni slices if want and cook the pizza for 5-10 minutes until cheese has melted.

COCONUT CHOCOLATE BARS

Ingredients:

1 cup shredded, unsweetened coconut

1 packet or 1/2 teaspoon Stevia

1 teaspoon vanilla extract

1/3 cup coconut cream

4 tablespoons coconut oil

2 tablespoons unsweetened cocoa powder

2 oz. cocoa butter

Instructions:

Mix shredded coconut with coconut cream, half of the vanilla extract and half of the Stevia. Blend well and place the mixture on a small cookie sheet lined with parchment paper. Shape the mixture into a rectangle and place in the freezer for two hours. Remove from the freezer and cut into five bars. While waiting for the bars to freeze cook the chocolate topping: melt coconut oil in a pan and add cocoa powder and remaining Stevia and vanilla extract. Mix on low heat for two minutes. Let the mixture cool to room temperature. Dip frozen bars into the chocolate and coat on both side. Place coated bars back on the cookie sheet and place in fridge until they harden and are ready to enjoy.

CRISPY AND CREAMY PANEER KEBABS

Ingredients:

100gms Paneer

25gms flaxseed powder

30ml coconut milk

3tsp ghee

1tbsp mint chutney

Instructions:

Cut paneer into thick slices.

Apply mint chutney on one side of two paneer slices and close like a sandwich.

Put coconut milk and flaxseed powder in two separate bowls.

Add salt and pepper to the flaxseed powder as per your taste.

Take each paneer sandwich and dip in coconut milk.

Dab coconut milk dipped paneer sandwich in flaxseed

powder on all sides.

Brush some ghee on the non stick grill pan and keep it on medium heat.

Place paneer slices on the heated grill and cook on medium heat.

Flip them over to cook from all sides.

Serve when paneer gets crispy with rich golden color from outside.

CRISPY PANEER KABAB

Ingredients:

1.5kg chicken broiler

150gms yogurt

5tsp ginger and garlic paste

30gms onion paste

15tsp ghee

1 cup cilantro or dhaniya leaves

30 gms curry leaves

1tsp mustard seeds

1tsp table salt

½ tsp pink salt

1tsp turmeric or haldi powder

1tsp red chili powder (optional)

2 to 3 green chillies (optional)

Instructions:

Wash chicken and pat dry.

Mix hung curd, turmeric powder, and both the salts. Marinate chicken evenly in that mixture.

Grind onions into fine paste and apply it to chicken. Let it set for 4-5 hours.

After 4-5 hours, heat ghee in the wok.

Add mustard seeds and let them splatter, add curry leaves on a medium heat.

Add chicken and continue cooking on medium heat.

After some time, chicken will start leaving water and will also appear a little tender.

Grind fresh cilantro or dhaniya with green chillies to make a fine paste using water.

Add this paste to the chicken and keep cooking for another 10-15 minutes.

Once all the water in chicken dries it means its cooked and ready for serving.

KETO BULLET PROOF COFFEE

Ingredients:

Instant coffee

Cooking coconut oil

Stevia drops

Instructions:

Boil a mug of water and add 1 tsp of instant coffee in it.

Once the coffee starts boiling, add half tsp coconut oil to it (you can add up to 1 tsp coconut oil as per your taste).

Let it simmer for a few mins before straining in a cup.

Add artificial sweetener of your choice and sip slowly.

Note: Coconut oil can be replaced with ghee or butter in the same quantity.

KETO SUPER ENERGY BAR

Ingredients:

100ml coconut oil

100gms almonds

30gms ground flax seeds

15gms chia seeds

1scoop MuscleBlaze Whey Protein Powder

pink salt (optional)

Instructions:

Place a thick bottomed pan on medium heat and pour coconut oil in it.

Grind almonds and put them in heated oil, keep stirring.

Add sweetener and keep stirring on low heat. If you feel that the oil is getting super hot, switch off the heat for three to four minutes.

Add grounded flax seeds and keep stirring.

At last add whey protein and stir to make mixture

look nice and sticky.

Add Chia seeds to the pan, mix well and remove from heat.

Line baking tin with parchment or butter paper and put the mixture in it.

Keep the tin in the deep freezer for at least two hours.

Once its set it will come out nicely from the tin.

Cut them into small cubes and store in an air tight container in refrigerator.

CABBAGE NOODLE TUNA CASSEROLE

Prep Time: 15 minutes

Cook Time: 30 minutes

Ingredients:

2 tbsp olive oil

2 tbsp grass-fed butter

medium head green cabbage (about 1 1/2 lbs), cut into large shreds

1 cup onion, chopped

3 ribs celery, chopped

2 cloves garlic, minced

sea salt and black pepper, to taste

2 tsp dried dill or 2 tbsp fresh dill

2 tsp dry mustard powder

2 tbsp lemon zest

juice of 1 lemon

1 1/2 cup heavy cream

1 1/4 cup Parmesan cheese, grated, divided

3 – 5oz cans albacore tuna, drained

1/2 cup frozen peas

Instructions:

Heat the olive oil and butter in an extra large ovenproof skillet over medium heat.

Once heated, add the cabbage, onion, celery, garlic, sea salt and black pepper to the pan.

Sauté until the vegetables are crisp tender – about 10 minutes.

Mix in the dill, mustard powder, lemon zest, and lemon juice.

Pour the heavy cream and 1 cup Parmesan cheese into the pan. Mix in and keep stirring until the cheese has melted and combined with the heavy cream.

Reduce heat to medium low and let simmer to allow the sauce to thicken.

Once the sauce has started to thicken, stir in the tuna

and the peas.

Sprinkle the remaining Parmesan over the top of the dish and transfer to the oven.

Broil on high for 3-5 minutes or until the Parmesan on top has made a golden brown crust.

KETO CHIPOTLE RED PEPPER CHEESE DIP

Preparation time: 10 minutes

Cooking time: 20 minutes

Total time: 30minutes

Ingredients (makes about 2 cups/ 6 servings):

3 medium red peppers, seeds and stalks removed (400 g/ 14 oz)

1 tbsp olive oil (15 ml)

1/4 cup sun-dried tomatoes (28 g/ 1 oz)

1/3 cup full-fat cream cheese (85 g/ 3 oz)

1 garlic clove, minced

1 tsp paprika

pinch of dried chipotle or chile flakes

sea salt, to taste

Optional: 1 tsp lemon juice, black pepper and chopped parsley

Instructions:

Preheat the oven to 200 °C/ 400 °F. Remove the stalk and seeds from the peppers. Chop into quarters and place on a baking tray. Drizzle with 1 tbsp of olive oil and roast in the oven for 15 minutes until soft. Keto Chipotle Red Pepper Cheese Dip

Immediately place in a sealable bag and allow to steam naturally for 3-5 minutes. This makes the skins easy to remove. Keto Chipotle Red Pepper Cheese Dip

Peel off the skins. Add the peppers, sun dried tomatoes, chipotle or chilli, paprika, cream cheese, garlic and salt to a mixing bowl. Keto Chipotle Red Pepper Cheese Dip

Blitz with a hand blender until smooth. Place in the fridge to thicken. Optionally, stir through 1 tsp of lemon juice before serving. Keto Chipotle Red Pepper Cheese Dip

Top with cracked black pepper and parsley if you prefer. Serve with crudités or keto crackers. Store in an airtight container in the fridge for up to 2 days.

LOW-CARB TURKISH EGGS

Turkish eggs are a popular breakfast recipe and a low-carb option made with kale and red onion.

Eggs should be part of a healthy keto diet - they are nature's perfect food. Eggs are zero-carb, high in micronutrients such as choline and vitamin B12, and they are also a good source of quality protein.

Kale is a great source of vitamin A, C and potassium and is perfect for those who watch their carb intake. Finally, avocado is the ultimate anti keto-flu food. It's one of the best sources of potassium, a good source of magnesium, and monounsaturated fats which are known to protect against heart disease.

The paprika, chili grass-fed butter drizzle makes it a flavour bomb against the soft egg yolks and creamy yogurt. A super easy, one pot classic that's perfect for a late brunch.

Hands-on: 20 minutes

Overall: 20 minutes

Ingredients (makes 4 servings):

Yogurt topping:

1/2 cup + 1 tbsp full-fat yogurt (140 g/ 5 oz)

1 tsp each lemon zest and lemon juice

1 garlic clove, minced

1 tbsp chopped cilantro

sea salt, to taste

1 tsp extra virgin olive oil

Eggs:

2 tbsp butter or ghee (28 g/ 1 oz)

1 medium red onion, sliced (100 g/ 3.5 oz)

200 g finely chopped kale (7 oz)

1 tbsp butter or ghee (14 g/ 0.5 oz)

4 large eggs

Spicy butter sauce:

2 tbsp butter or ghee (28 g/ 1 oz)

1/2 tsp paprika

1 tsp chili or tomato flakes

Topping:

1/2 medium avocado, sliced (75 g/ 2.5 oz)

1/4 tsp black pepper

chili flakes and sea salt, to taste

2 tbsp pine nuts (17 g/ 0.6 oz)

Instructions:

Mix all the yogurt ingredients together in a small bowl and set aside: yogurt, lemon juice and zest, garlic, cilantro, salt and olive oil.

Heat 1 oz butter in a cast iron pan. Fry the onions on a low-medium heat for 2 minutes until soft.

Add the kale and cook for a further 2 minutes. Stir to combine.

Make 4 wells in the mixture. Add a small knob of butter (total of about 1/2 oz) to each hole to prevent sticking.

Crack open the eggs, one into each well. Allow to cook for 6 – 8 minutes until the egg whites are set and the yolks soft, or to your liking. Remove from the heat.

In a separate saucepan, melt the remaining 1 oz butter and add the paprika, chilli or tomato flakes and a pinch of salt. Simmer for 30 seconds until bubbling. Remove from the heat.

Top the eggs with sliced avocado and yogurt.

 Drizzle with spiced butter and sprinkle with pine nuts. Season with extra salt, pepper and chili flakes.

Drizzle with Sriracha sauce and serve immediately!

SHRIMP TACO BOWLS

Prep Time 15 minutes

Cook Time 5 minutes

Total Time 20 minutes

Ingredients:

Marinade:

1 lb medium shrimp peeled and deveined

2 tbsp lemon juice

2 cloves garlic crushed

1 tsp cumin

1/8 teaspoon chili powder

1 tbsp olive oil

1/2 tsp salt

To Serve:

cilantro leaves

1 avocado chopped

Mango salsa:

1/2 mango chopped

1 cup cherry tomatoes

1/2 cup red onion chopped

2 tsp lime juice, or to taste salt, to taste

Instructions:

Peel and devein the shrimp.

Add the peeled deveined shrimp to the shrimp taco bowl marinade for 15 minutes.

In the same pan add the shrimp and cook for about two minutes per side or until they turn pink.

Serve with chopped avocado, and make a simple mango salsa with the mango, tomatoes, and onion.

BLACKENED SHRIMP

Prep Time: 5 minutes

Cook Time: 5 minutes

Total Time: 10 minutes

Servings: 4

Calories: 175 kcal

Ingredients:

1 lb shrimp peeled, deveined

3 tbsp homemade Blackened Seasoning

2 tbsp olive oil

Instructions:

Toss peeled and deveined shrimp with the blackened seasoning and let sit in the fridge for 10-15 minutes.

Heat the oil in a wide skillet.

Cook the shrimp for about 2 minutes and then turn them over for a couple more minutes until they are cooked all the way through, they will turn pink/white color when they are done.

PARMESAN CARROTS

Prep Time: 10 minutes

Cook Time: 20 minutes

Total Time: 30 minutes

Ingredients:

1 lb carrots peeled and cut into sticks

2 tbsp olive oil

2 cloves garlic crushed

1/4 tsp black pepper ground

1/2 tsp salt

3 tbsp Parmesan cheese grated

Instructions:

Preheat the oven to 400F.

Line a sheet pan with parchment paper.

Toss carrots in olive oil, garlic, salt and pepper.

Bake for 15 minutes then sprinkle on the Parmesan cheese.

Bake for a further 5-10 minutes until carrots are soft and the cheese is melted.

Remove from the oven and serve hot.

CHICKEN AVOCADO SALAD

This Chicken Avocado Salad with Honey-Lime Dressing is such a fun summer salad! It's jam-packed with healthy ingredients including arugula, spinach, and mango.

Prep Time: 10 minutes

Cook Time: 10 minutes

Total Time: 20 minutes

Ingredients:

2 cups Romaine lettuce

1 cup arugula

1 cup baby spinach

1 avocado

1/2 English cucumber

1 cup cherry tomatoes

1 cup mango

1/2 cup red onion chopped

Chicken marinade:

4 chicken thighs skinless and boneless

1 lime zest from one lime

3 tbsp fresh lime juice approx two limes

3 tbsp olive oil

4 cloves garlic crushed

2 tsp oregano

1/2 tsp salt

1/2 tsp pepper

Honey-lime dressing:

3 tablespoons olive oil

2 tbsp fresh lime juice approx 1 lime

2 tsp honey

1/2 tsp salt

1/8th tsp cayenne pepper

Instructions:

Mix together the grilled chicken marinade and pour over the chicken. Marinate for 1 hour.

Cook the chicken on a grill or in a cast iron grill pan with a little oil on a medium heat until it's cooked all the way through.

To make the honey-lime dressing mix all the ingredients together to combine. taste and adjust the seasonings and honey if you need to.

Assemble your chicken avocado salad by adding the romaine lettuce, arugula, baby spinach, grilled chicken, avocado, cucumber, cherry tomatoes, mango, and red onion into a large bowl. Add as much salad dressing as you like, then toss salad.

ULTIMATE KETO BUNS

Hands-on: 10-15 minutes

Overall: 55-60 minutes

Ingredients (makes 10 buns):

Dry ingredients:

1 1/2 cup almond flour (almond meal) (150 g/ 5.3 oz)

2/3 cup psyllium husks - will be powdered, or 1/3 cup psyllium husk powder (40 g/ 1.4 oz)

1/2 cup coconut flour (60 g/ 2.1 oz)

1/2 packed cup flax meal (75 g/ 2.6 oz)

2 tsp garlic powder

2 tsp onion powder

2 tsp cream of tartar or apple cider vinegar

1 tsp baking soda

1 tsp pink Himalayan or sea salt

5 tbsp sesame seeds (or sunflower, flax, poppy seeds)

or 1-2 tbsp caraway seeds

Optional: 1-2 tbsp Erythritol or Swerve

Wet ingredients:

6 large egg whites

2 large eggs

2 cups water, boiling or lukewarm depending on the method - see intro (480 ml/ 16 fl oz)

Tips & substitutions:

If making a loaf instead of buns, bake for 75 minutes! Do not use a silicon loaf pan - use a metallic one instead.

Flax-free, multi-purpose bread, includes a nut-free option.

Nut-free keto buns - include flaxmeal

If you don't want to use coconut flour: use twice the amount of almond flour or flaxmeal instead of coconut flour (1 cup of almond flour/flaxmeal instead of 1/2 cup coconut flour). Or you can use the same amount but reduce the water by 1/2 cup.

If using apple cider vinegar instead of cream of tartar, make sure to mix it with the wet ingredients.

For best results, use a kitchen scale when measuring all the dry ingredients. Using just cups may not be enough to achieve best results, especially in baked goods. Weights per cups and tablespoons may vary depending on the product/ brand or if you make you own ingredients (like flaxmeal from flaxseeds). Psyllium absorbs lots of water.

When baking with psyllium, you must remember to drink enough water throughout the day to prevent constipation.

Instructions:

Preheat the oven to 175 °C/ 350 °F. Use a kitchen scale to measure all the ingredients and add them to a mixing bowl (apart from the sesame seeds which are used for topping): almond flour, coconut flour, flax meal, psyllium husk powder, garlic powder, onion powder, cream of tartar, baking soda, salt (and optionally, Erythritol).

Do not use whole psyllium husks - if you cannot find psyllium husk powder, use a blender or coffee grinder and process until fine. If you get already prepared psyllium husk powder, remember to weigh it before adding to the recipe. I used whole psyllium husks which I powdered myself. Do not use just measuring cups - different products have different weights per cup!

Mix all the dry ingredients.

Cream of tartar and baking soda act as leavening agents. This is how it works: To get 2 teaspoons of gluten-free baking powder, you need 1/2 a teaspoon of baking soda and 1 teaspoon of cream of tartar (double in this recipe of 10 buns). If you don't have cream of tartar, instead you can use apple cider vinegar and add it to the wet ingredients.

Erythritol could be omitted in this recipe - the effect on carbs is minimum. It works in two ways: it acts as leavening agent and creates the slightly sweet taste burger buns have. Also, if you don't have both onion and garlic powder, you can use just one of them or use freshly mashed garlic cloves (2 cloves per recipe of 5 buns).

Add the egg whites and eggs. and process well using a mixer until the dough is thick.

The reason you shouldn't use only whole eggs is that the buns wouldn't rise with so many egg yolks in.

Don't waste them - use them for making Home-made Mayo, Easy Hollandaise Sauce or Lemon Curd.

Add boiling water and process until well combined.

Using a spoon, make the buns and place them on a non-stick baking tray or a parchment paper. They will grow in size, so make sure to leave some space between them. You can even use small tart trays.

Top each of the buns with sesame seeds (or any other seeds) and press them into the dough, so they don't fall out. Place in the oven and cook for 45-50 minutes.

Remove from the oven, let the tray cool down and place the buns on a rack to cool down to room temperature. Store them at room temperature if you plan to use them in the next couple of days or store in the freezer for future use.

Top with butter or cream cheese, burger meat or any topping you like.

Tip: To save time, mix all the dry ingredients ahead and store in a zip-lock bag and add a label with the number of servings. When ready to be baked, just add the wet ingredients!

Suggestions:

If for any reason you can't get this recipe to work,

here are some tips that might help. Most of the above tips apply to any recipes using psyllium husk powder:

Make sure you weigh all the ingredients using scales. Even small differences can affect the final result of this recipe.

If the buns appear to have large hollow bubbles inside, it may be due to the psyllium. Make sure you use powder, not whole husks. Otherwise, use a coffee grinder or blender and pulse until fine and powdery.

For a slightly (but not significantly) better result, incorporate the eggs separately. First, whisk the egg whites until they create soft peaks and add cream of tartar used in this recipe. In another bowl, mix the egg yolks and gently fold them into the egg whites. In a separate bowl, mix the dry ingredients and pour in the hot water. Process well using an electric mixer (hand whisk is not as good in this recipe). Add the foamy egg white mixture into the batter and process well. Try not to deflate the batter completely. Form the buns and place in the oven.

If the buns don't rise properly, use only egg whites and omit the egg yolks.

If the final result is too moist, do not reduce the

water used in this recipe or the psyllium will clump. Instead, dry the buns in the oven on low, up to 100 °C/ 210 °F for 30-60 minutes. If needed, cut them in half and place in a toaster.

Do not leave the batter outside the oven for too long. Place in the oven as soon as you form the buns.

If the buns change color to slight purple, it's due to the psyllium husk powder. Whenever I use whole husks and grind them at home, they are always perfect, light brown. However, when I use ready-made psyllium husk powder, they look purple, especially the next day. Although they may not look appetising, they are perfectly fine.

KETO RASPBERRY LEMON LOAF

Hands-on: 10 minutes

Overall: 1 hour 10 minutes

Ingredients (10 servings):

Loaf:

3 large eggs

1 large egg white

juice and zest from 1 lemon

1/4 cup melted butter, ghee or virgin coconut oil (60 ml/ 2 fl oz)

1 1/2 cups almond flour (150 g/ 5.3 oz)

3/4 cup powdered Swerve (108 g/ 3.8 oz)

1/4 tsp sea salt

1 tsp baking powder

1 cup fresh raspberries (120 g/ 4.2 oz)

Glaze & topping:

1/2 cup powdered Swerve (80 g/ 2.8 oz)

juice and zest from 1 lemon

1/2 cup fresh raspberries (62 g/ 2.2 oz)

Note: The glaze is very sweet and may be too sweet for those who are used to low-carb eating. Alternatively, you can use the glaze in our Low-Carb Lemon Cake which is made with melted coconut butter, coconut oil, lemon juice and lemon zest (sweetener can be skipped or used to taste).

Instructions:

Preheat oven to 175 °C/ 350 °F and line a loaf pan with parchment paper.

In a large bowl whisk together the dry cake ingredients. In another bowl, beat the eggs using a hand mixer.

Add the melted butter (or ghee), lemon juice, and lemon zest.

Gently fold in the raspberries and mix using a spatula.

Pour into the loaf pan lined with parchment paper and spread evenly using a spatula.

Bake for 1 hour or until a toothpick inserted into the center comes out clean. Once cooked, remove from the oven, set aside and let cool before adding the glaze.

To make the glaze simply mix together the ingredients in a small bowl until smooth.

Pour over the cooled loaf.

Sprinkle with the reserved raspberries.

Slice and serve. Store covered in the refrigerator for up to 5 days.

CONCLUSION

Start burning fat today without more exercise! Take control of your metabolism naturally by adopting a ketogenic diet plan. Your body was designed for this style of nutrition. Your metabolic state can be optimized by consuming the (delicious) foods that our genetic forefathers thrived on, and this does not include carbohydrate-rich, processed foods loaded with sugars and bad fats. It involves a luxurious and fulfilling diet based on bountiful foods from paleolithic times, including lean meats, vegetables, nuts and seeds, and healthy fats that your body will thank you for.

Virtually all weight loss diets to varying degrees focus on either calorie reduction or the manipulation of the intake of one of the three essential macronutrients (proteins, fats, or carbohydrates) to achieve their weight loss effects.

Ketogenic diets are a group of "high-fat, moderate protein" or "high-protein moderate fat" but very low-carbohydrate diets. The term ketogenic basically refers to the increased production of ketone bodies occasioned by the elevated rate of lipolysis (fat break down). Ketones are acidic by-products formed during the intermediate break down of "fat" into "fatty acids" by the liver.

Despite the ability of ketogenic diets to reduce insulin production, their main objective is ultimately aimed at inducing the state of ketosis. Ketosis can be regarded as a condition or state in which the rate of formation of ketones produced by the break-down of "fat" into "fatty acids" by the liver is greater than the ability of tissues to oxidize them. Ketosis is actually a secondary state of the process of lipolysis (fat break down) and is a general side effect of low-carbohydrate diets. Ketogenic diets are therefore favorably disposed to the encouragement and promotion of ketosis.

Prolonged periods of starvation can easily induce ketosis, but they can also be deliberately induced by making use of a low-calorie or low-carbohydrate diet through the ingestion of large amounts of either fats or proteins and drastically reduced carbohydrates. Therefore, high-fat and high-protein diets are the weight loss diets used to deliberately induce ketosis.

Essentially, ketosis is a very efficient form of energy production which does not involve the production of insulin as the body rather burns its fat deposits for energy. Consequently, the idea of reducing carbohydrate consumption does not only reduce insulin production but also practically forces the body to burn its fat deposit for energy, thereby making use of ketogenic diets is a very powerful way to achieve rapid weight loss.

Ketogenic diets are designed in such a way that they initially force the body to exhaust its glucose supply and then finally switch to burning its fat deposits for energy. Subsequent food intakes after inducing the state of ketosis are meant to keep the ketosis process running by appropriately adjusting further carbohydrate consumption to provide just the basic amount of calories needed by the body.

KETOGENIC VEGETARIAN

INTRODUCTION

A ketogenic diet is one that requires us to reduce the number of calories we eat to below the amount of calories our bodies use in a day, triggering the release of energy that is stored as fat in our body's cells. This fat is also called ketones, which our muscles use as fuel. Of course, there is a big difference between starving yourself and simply reducing your caloric intake in a way that keeps you satisfied and healthy.

This book illustrates the idea that long term success at maintaining fat loss requires that we feel good during and after weight loss. Maintaining steady energy levels, keeping your moods stable, and the fun and excitement of creating your own desired changes are the keys to your success.

This type of ketogenic diet does not mean over-eating huge slabs of meat. Likewise, it does it mean over-indulging in fried or fatty foods or completely eliminating carbohydrates.

Some people have misused the idea of low-carb ketogenic diets by misinterpreting the intention of clinicians who promote this method. As a result, the media as well as some medical authorities have emphasize the "dangers" or "failures" that have followed the extreme behaviors adopted by some people. In fact, this book overwhelmingly shows that a low-carb ketogenic diet is not only safe, but is also effective for fat loss.

As you read, you will also learn more about the following...

1. Delicious and healthy recipes for rapid weight loss
2. What a Ketogenic Vegetarian Diet is
3. Why we should follow a Ketogenic Vegetarian Diet
4. Delicious and easy Ketogenic Vegetarian recipes
5. How we eat to lose weight
6. Ketosis is not a ketoacidosis
7. Whether or not a Vegetarian Ketogenic Diet is possible
8. Recommended and advisable foods
9. Fat for vegetarians in ketosis
10. Protein sources on a Vegetarians Ketogenic Diet

Using this book is best for you and your family.

CHAPTER ONE

WHAT IS KETOGENIC VEGETARIAN DIET

Not everyone with PCOS is obviously overweight, however, the health of everyone with PCOS is threatened by the body chemistry that results from eating either a standard America diet, or a standard vegetarian diet.

PCOS is a version of what is also known as Metabolic Syndrome, or Syndrome X. This is the condition that results in men, women, and (sadly) in more and more children in recent years. This condition is a result of overeating foods that are highly processed, artificially flavored and preserved, high refined flour and full of simple carbohydrates.

The excess of sweets, breads, pastas, cereals, and packaged foods provides many more calories than the average person uses in a day. Even organically grown grains, eaten whole or manufactured into "wholesome" forms of old favorites like chips, cookies, etc., will have the same effect as excess sugar when over eaten. The insulin required to process all the blood sugar that results from diets that are high in sugar, flour, etc., is what causes higher levels of testosterone in women.

Increased levels of testosterone can then lead to hormone imbalances which cause polycystic ovaries, infertility, acne, facial hair, and hair thinning. Left unchanged, this diet caneventually cause obesity, diabetes, and heart disease; it creates a higher risk for certain cancers as well.

Foods high in carbohydrates can lead to:

- Elevated insulin levels

- Elevated testosterone levels

- Menstrual disorders

- Facial and body hair darkening and becoming coarse

- Hair thinning on the scalp

- Acne

- Increased risk for infertility, obesity, diabetes, heart disease, and certain cancers

Once you have extra fat, you have to eat in a special way for what I call a "therapeutic interval". This simply means that there are certain changes that you have to make and a certain amount of time is required for fat loss to be fully successful. This special way of eating does not have to be the way you will eat the rest of your life... IF you include building muscle and using your muscle while losing this fat. The more muscle you have, the more calories you must consume to be healthy. Similarly, with little muscle and not much exercise, there is not much you can eat without your body storing fat.

How We Eat to Lose Weight

The most reliable and straightforward way to use up stored fat is through a diet that eliminates unnecessary sweets and starchy carbohydrates while also providing plenty of fresh, whole vegetables, fruit, nuts, good quality oils and lean, clean animal protein.

Almost every successful weight loss diet is a ketogenic diet. A ketogenic diet is where we reduce our total caloric intake to below the amount of calories our bodies use in a day, triggering the release of energy stored as fat in our body cells. This fat is in the form of chemistry called ketones, which our muscles use as fuel. Of course, there is a big difference between starving yourself and reducing your calories in a way that keeps you satisfied and healthy!

Ultimately our long term success at maintaining fat loss requires that we feel good during and after weight loss. Maintaining steady energy levels, keeping your moods stable, and the fun and excitement of creating your own desired changes are the keys to your success.

It turns out that you can burn more fat while eating a larger number of calories when you get fewer of your calories from carbohydrates and more from good, quality protein and fat. This type of ketogenic diet does not mean over-eating huge slabs of meat. Likewise, it does not mean over-indulging in fried or fatty foods or completely eliminating carbohydrates.

Some people have misused the idea of low-carb ketogenic diets by misinterpreting the intention of clinicians who promote this method. As a result, the media as well as some medical authorities have emphasize the "dangers" or "failures" that have followed the extreme behaviors adopted by some people. In fact, this book overwhelmingly shows that a low-carb ketogenic diet is not only safe, but is also effective for fat loss.

Remember, we can only lose fat by reducing our caloric intake to less than the amount of calories we use in our daily activities. This is a fundamental truth. However, there are many additional details that make this strategy more or less likely to succeed, especially over time. Some conditions that complicate the basic calories-fat-reduced equation include:

– Chronic stress that fatigues your adrenal

function

- Chronic pain that keeps your nervous system on high alert

- Insomnia that reduces the opportunity for your organs to perform restorative functions that will not happen except during deep sleep

- Perimenopause or other conditions that alter your reproductive hormone functions (including the use of contraceptive hormones, hormone replacement therapy, a hysterectomy, and breastfeeding)

- Thyroid disorders

- Kidney disease

- Any immobilizing condition

All of these conditions can be addressed with a diet plan as well as a transition plan that is personalized to your situation.

One important detail to our weight loss success has to do with how we feel physically, mentally, and emotionally when we reduce calories. If we simply eat less without regarding the composition of our diet, i.e., the fat, protein, and carbohydrate content as well as the vitamins and minerals that we need, chances are that we will have an unpleasant experience. This is because hunger, fatigue, headaches, muscle spasms, mental fogginess, depression, irritability, and insomnia are common experiences shared by dieters who use low fat, low calorie, high carbohydrate diets. With these diets, we can also find ourselves losing weight that includes muscle mass along with fat we wanted to lose.

In a low-carb ketogenic diet, we reduce our calories from starchy carbohydrates in particular and nourish our selves with appropriate amounts of water, vegetables, fruit, eggs, poultry, fish, meat, nuts, and good quality oils. This change helps to creates fat loss without the usual unpleasant side effects. It also helps us to identify problem foods, so that when we transition from a fat loss diet to a more "natural" diet to maintain weight, we can do so without returning to old food-related problems.

CHAPTER TWO

KETOSIS IS NOT KETOACIDOSIS

Ketones are a product of fat metabolism and function as a source of energy for the body. Our muscles as well as other tissues can use ketones for fuel instead of glucose, or blood sugar. Ketones are released from stored fat and then used for energy when there is not enough glucose available. This is because our brains require blood sugar for fuel whereas muscles and other metabolic processes can take up ketones instead. Additionally, we can make blood glucose from everything we eat, including by transforming proteins from animal foods. We can not, however, make protein for our bodies from plant foods. Rather, what we end up making from the carbohydrates of plant food is fat. The excess carbohydrates we eat every day beyond what we use when exercising our muscles is transformed into and stored as fat. This was a great system for people (like our human ancestors) who do not have a reliable food supply and are subject to regular periods of feast or famine. For most of us, however, it means that we have an ever enlarging "storage bin" of accumulated fat.

There is some confusion regarding the ketosis that occurs when we are eating fewer carbohydrates than we need for daily fuel and begin to burn stored fat instead. Some people confuse normal, beneficial ketosis with something known as ketoacidosis which occurs when people with high blood sugar levels i.e., diabetics, simultaneously produce high levels of ketones.

People with diabetes do not produce enough insulin from their pancreas, or they have a condition called insulin resistance which is when tissues no longer respond to the presence of insulin bearing glucose that is being delivered into storage. Ketones are formed in response to the tissues need for some fuel other than the glucose, which is collecting in the blood attached to insulin molecules but can no longer be delivered into cells. Generally, our bodies will adjust the blood pH level to balance this shifting chemistry; however, in diabetics, the imbalance is too great causing ketoacidosis, or increased acidity of the blood to occur. Metabolic ketoacidosis in people with diabetes is a dangerous condition and should be avoided with very strict control and attention to diet as well as blood sugar levels.

When a person with normal blood sugar levels produces ketones by breaking down fat for fuel while not eating excess carbohydrates, blood glucose is delivered elegantly, primarily to the brain, and the rest of the body happily uses ketones to run the show.

Eating foods that are rich in carbohydrates in amounts that allow for the release of ketones from stored fat is a safe and effective way to reduce body fat while maintaining an even blood sugar levels. Keeping your blood sugar levels stable means you will have plenty of physical energy, be mentally alert, and experience restful sleep. Most people can eat this way for the rest of their lives and be quite well, and most people will actually want to diversify their diet after having lost excess fat. Expanding your diet to include more fruits, grains, and appropriate celebratory treats can be accomplished without regaining fat.

This transition has to be done thoughtfully and with close attention to the impact of certain foods. For example, some people will never be able to eat certain foods without experienceing negative consequences because of their genetic make up. Regardless, we all have to reintroduce foods carefully and maintain exercise throughout our lives in order not to regain lost fat.

A ketogenic fat loss diet is not appropriate for pregnancy and breastfeeding as these are times when fat stores are very important to the wellbeing of both the mother and her baby/babies. Additionally, people with kidney damage, diabetes, epilepsy, and gall bladder problems should not use this diet unless they will be closely supervised by their physician.

Women lose weight somewhat slower than men because feminine hormones, i.e., estrogen, effects how women hold onto water and fat. In general, men have greater muscle mass, even when quite fat. In addition to hormones such as testosterone, this help them burn fat somewhat more effectively than women. Regardless, regular exercise is absolutely necessary for everyone's long term health.

How we transition from fat loss to long term healthy diet determines our long term success.

Transitioning successfully from a fat loss diet to a healthy life long diet is only beginning to be understood. Specifics for success include:

- A metabolic readjustment period (5 to 10 or more weeks)

- Educational support that works with the habits of thought and feelings surrounding body image and our learned eating and exercise behaviors.

Whenever we let go of stored energy (a.k.a. fat) by reducing our caloric intake, primitive protective mechanisms in our brains kick in and our basic metabolic rate starts to slow down. When this happens, our bodies actually start using less fat to protect us from what our ancestrial hard-wired brain thinks is a famine. For our human ancestors, an unreliable food supply made this trait essential for survival. For those of us who are eating less by choice, however, this mechanism is what will cause us to regain weight we have lost as soon as we start eating "normally" again.

That "normal" eating concept is key. If you get fat, then you need to eat to lose fat, but when you have reached your goal weight, you resume eating the way you did that got you fat in the first place and the cycle continues like that. Not only are you eating the same food that caused you to gain weight again, you are piling it into a body that is newly programmed to burn less energy during your regular daily activities. In some cases, you may also have have lost muscle mass. In order to complete the change to a forever-leaner you, fat loss is truly only step one.

Step two is working to re-set your metabolic rate to where is was or higher than it was before you began your fat loss diet. How that is done is a mystery that has frustrated the many dieters; it has also caused a great deal of unhealthy and frustrating yo-yo patterns of weight loss and regain.

We know that 90% of people who lose weight regain what they lost and then some. However, some people do not regain weight and recent research has examined what is different about this fascinating 10%. Essentially what these folks do differently is they become acutely aware of small amounts weight regained, and they return to their weight loss behaviors for brief periods of time to lose what they have regained. Eventually, as long as they maintain consistently healthy habits, including their food choices and exercise levels, the episodes of weight gain stop and they stabilize at their new weight.

Transitioning to healthy eating after losing weight requires:

- Having an established, regular, and fun exercise habit once you arrive at your goal weight

- Keeping very close tabs on your weight as well as on your inches at your waist and hips

- Returning to weight loss behaviors whenever you have regained 2 to 3 pounds.

- After returning to weight loss behaviors, expand your food choices again until you eventually stabilize at yous goal weight with your new commitment to and enjoyment of regular exercise.

— Continue maintaining a healthy muscle mass, activity level, and consistently adjust your diet to one that consists of fresh, whole foods as you age and/or encounter new circumstances or health challenges

Remember – there is one proven way that we need to eat to lose fat, and another more generous and complex way we can eat once our goal is attained. The nature of the transition between these two ways of eating is essential to long term success. However, the ability to lose weight, make dietary changes that are less stringent and more varied, then return as often as needed to the weight loss regime for brief periods until stabilized, is apparently a rare ability. Most people do not seem to discover this behavior spontaneously. Thus, long term guidance and support is crucial.

A number of studies on successful weight loss have clarified that knowledgeable support helps people to not only remember the basic, straightforward steps of the diet cha-cha, but also helps them expand their skills for stress management, exercise options, and cooking skills. Often times, the benefits and habits that are leaned during this process benefit everyone around you, including your family.

We have many behaviors and beliefs that affect our sense of self and our ability to pursue long-term self-discipline. It is clear that ongoing and specific support, in the form of individual counseling or a similar support group experience, makes success much more likely. We encourage you to use both the weight loss and maintenance aspects of the program described here, while also adding in regular exercise and regular contact with a knowledgeable and/or skilled support system to ensure long term results.

CHAPTER THREE

IS A KETOGENIC DIET FOR VEGETARIANS REASONABLY POSSIBLE?

Regardless of your motives for cutting out animal meat, you are probably equally aware of all the buzz about the ketogenic diet and wondering if you can go keto while staying away from all meats.

The answer is "yes", but it takes a little extra thought. While the traditional keto diet typically involves a lot of meat for protein, it's not necessary to eat meat while following the plan. In fact, the biggest component of the ketogenic diet is good fat, which you can easily get from vegetarian foods.

For omnivores going keto, the most common mistake is eating too much protein.

Similarly, the biggest mistake that vegetarians make whengoing keto is eating too many carbohydrates from vegetables. You do have to be a little more careful with your carb and protein choices since traditional vegetarian forms of protein include things like beans and grains, which aren't a part of a keto diet.

Let's tackle this by discussing the three

macronutrients one at a time.

Carbohydrates for a Vegetarian Ketogenic Diet

Since vegetarian diets are typically higher in carbs than carnivorous diets, it's especially important to understand the "right" types of carbs when following a vegetarian2 ketogenic diet.

Good Carbs vs. Bad Carbs

Besides getting plenty of healthy fats, watching your carb intake is one of the most important factors here—and many go-to meals, especially snacks common for vegetarians and vegans, are pretty carb-heavy. However, to reiterate, excessive carbohydrates (even from veggies) aren't part of a keto diet and ff course, refined carbs like sugar, flour, bread, cereal, chips, etc. are immediately off the table.

Bad Carbs (High Glycemic; Highly Processed)

Here are some carb sources to remove from your home and kitchen:

- Pastas

- Breads

- Chips, crackers, and pretzels

- Tortillas

- Rice

- Sodas

- Cereals

- Packaged foods with refined sugars or flours

- Fruit juices and most fruits

- White potatoes and sweet potatoes

- Starchy vegetables

Good carbs on a vegetarian keto diet are basically the same as those on a normal keto diet including low-carb fruits, full-fat yogurts, and low-carb veggies.

Good Carbs (Limited) for a Vegetarian on Keto

Low-carb Vegetables

If you're one of those vegetarians who hates vegetables, this diet is going to be harder for you. While the most important aspect of keto is keeping your fat content high, you'll need healthy low-carb veggies to provide enough bulk and fiber to fill in your meals and get enough to eat.

Don't be afraid to explore and open yourself up to trying new vegetables in different ways. For instance, if raw veggies turn you off, try cooking some in coconut oil or butter with herbs and/or seasonings. Give yourself time to get used to the changes. Here are some low-carb vegetables to rely on:

- Spinach
- Kale
- Collard greens
- Swiss chard
- Lettuce
- Asparagus
- Green beans
- Broccoli
- Cucumber
- Summer and winter squash
- Red and white cabbage
- Cauliflower
- Bell peppers
- Onions
- Mushrooms
- Tomatoes
- Eggplants
- Garlic

Fruits

As a general rule, all fruits should be limited, however, berries are lower in sugars and carbs so they're typically okay in small amounts and at the end of the day before you fast while sleeping:

- Blackberries
- Strawberries
- Raspberries
- Blueberries

Non-Carbs to Mention (Condiments and Spices)

Spices

- Basil
- Oregano
- Parsley
- Rosemary
- Thyme
- Cilantro

- Cayenne pepper

- Chili powder

- Cumin

- Cinnamon

- Nutmeg

- Lemon or lime juice

- Pepper and salt

Protein on a Vegetarian Ketogenic Diet

Here's a comprehensive list of foods which contain protein that have the green light on a keto vegetarian diet:

Vegetarian Ketogenic Proteins

- Eggs

- Dairy

- Tempeh

- Natto

- Miso

- Nuts and seeds

If you do choose to eat soy products at all, try to stick to only those that are non-GMO and fermented (like organic tempeh).

If you find your protein needs still aren't being met, consider using an organic rice or hemp protein powder, but only use it as a supplement and not a regular meal replacement. Additionally, just remember that getting too much protein is a common ketogenic diet mistake that prevents your body from entering ketosis.

Be wary of packaged vegan and vegetarian meat substitutes, for while these might be good substitutes for meat in terms of fat and protein, they might also contain a high amount of carbs. Be sure to check the ingradients as well as the carb content per serving. Is it full or preservatives and fillers? If so, better meat substitutes would be any of the proteins mentioned above as well as portobello mushrooms or eggplant.

Fats for Vegetarians in Ketosis

Nuts and Seeds

Nuts and seeds are great sources of protein and fat, just be sure to choose mostly low-carb and high-fat choices because some nuts and seeds are higher in carbs than others and can add up quickly. Check out our full guide to nuts on the ketogenic diet and recipes like our insanely easy Macadamia Nut Fat Bomb.

Best nut options (low carb):

- Pecans

- Brazil nuts

- Macadamia nuts

- Walnuts

- Coconut (unsweetened)

- Hazelnuts

- Pine nuts

- Almonds

- Nut butters made from any of the above

Ketogenic Diet for Vegetarians

Nut options to eat sparingly or not at all (high carb):

- Peanuts

- Pistachios

- Cashews

- Chestnuts

Best seed options:

- Chia seeds

- Flaxseeds

Healthy Oils

The right types of oils are great for a ketogenic diet because they're entirely made of fat. MCT's in particular are a type of fat that metabolizes quicker than most and then broken down into useable energy. It also can easily cross the blood-brain barrier, which is why they are so beneficial to our mental clarity and performance. Here are some more great options:

- Olive oil

- Coconut oil

- Avocado oil

- MCT oil

- Macadamia oil

- Flaxseed oil

Other Non-Dair Fat Sources

- Olives

- Avocados

- Cocoa butter

- Coconut cream

Dairy and Eggs

- Heavy whipping cream

- Cream cheese

- Cottage cheese

- Mayonnaise

- Hard cheeses like parmesan, swiss, feta, and cheddar (full-fat)

- Soft cheese like brie, Monterrey jack, mozzarella, and bleu cheese (full-fat)

- Butter (grass-fed)

- Eggs (pastured or free-range and preferably omega-3-enriched)

- Full-fat unsweetened Greek yogurt or coconut yogurt

Breakfasts Ideas

- Vegetables and eggs with avocado fried in coconut or olive oil

- Egg frittata with asparagus and avocado

- Vegetable and feta omelet fried in coconut or olive oil

- Smoothie made from coconut cream, berries, ice, full-fat yogurt, almond butter, and stevia extract

Lunch Ideas

- Egg and avocado salad

- Mixed greens salad with avocado, mozzarella, pesto, olives, bell pepper, onions, nuts, lemon juice, and extra virgin olive oil dressing

- Vegetarian low-carb Greek salad with feta, tomatoes, onions, olives, fresh Greek spices, and extra virgin olive oil

- Stir-fried cauliflower "rice" with veggies and eggs

Dinner Ideas

- Cheese pizza with cauliflower crust and broccoli

VEGETARIAN KETO CLUB SALAD

Ingredients

2 tbsp sour cream

2 tbsp mayonnaise

1/2 tsp garlic powder

1/2 tsp onion powder

1 tsp dried parsley

1 tbsp milk

3 large hard boiled eggs, sliced

4 ounces cheddar cheese, cubed

3 cups romaine lettuce, torn into pieces

1/2 cup cherry tomatoes, halved

1 cup diced cucumber

1 tbsp dijon mustard

Directions

Prepare the dressing by mixing the sour cream, mayonnaise, and dried herbs until combined.

Add one tbsp of milk and mix. If the dressing seems too thick,feel free to add another tbsp of milk but don't forget to add another tbsp of milk to the final fat/protein/carb count if you do!

Layer your salad with the fresh veggies, cheese, and sliced egg. Add a spoonful of Dijon mustard in the center.

Drizzle with the prepared dressing, about 2 tbsp for one serving, then toss to coat.

NOATMEAL

Ingredients

1/2 cup (120 ml) water (see Note)

2 tbsp hemp hearts

2 tbsp almond flour

2 tbsp unsweetened shredded coconut

1 tbsp flaxseed meal

1 tbsp chia seeds

1/4 tsp granulated stevia (or any kind of sweetener you like to taste)

1 pinch sea salt

1/2 tsp pure vanilla extract

Directions

Stove top Directions Add all ingredients except for the vanilla to a small saucepan over low heat. Cook until thickened, stirring constantly, about 3 to 5 minutes. Stir in the vanilla and serve warm.

Microwave Directions Add all ingredients except for the vanilla to a large cereal bowl that's microwave-safe. Microwave on high until thickened, about 2 minutes. Stir in the vanilla and serve warm.

KETO OVERNIGHT "OATS"

Ingredients

Vanilla Keto Overnight Oats

⅔ cup (160 ml) full-fat coconut milk (plus more for the following day)

1/2 cup (75 grams) Manitoba Harvest Hemp Hearts

1 tbsp chia seed

2 tsps confectioners' erythritol or 3 to 4 drops of liquid stevia

1/2 tsp vanilla extract

A pinch of finely ground Himalayan rock salt

Optional Toppings

12 whole almonds, omit for nut-free

6 whole raspberries

Directions

Add all ingredients to a 12 fl. oz. (350 ml), or larger container with a lid and stir until combined. Cover and set in the fridge overnight, for at least 8 hours.

The following day, add additional milk until desired consistency is reached.

Divide between two small bowls, add toppings if desired.

CHIA SEED PUDDING RECIPE

Ingredients

2 cups coconut milk (homemade or natural)

1/2 cup Chia Seeds

1/2 tsp vanilla extract

1/4 cup (or less) maple syrup (or sub any sweetener)

Optional: 1/4 tsp cinnamon powder

Directions

For Blended/Smooth Version: Place all ingredients in a blender and blend on high for 1-2 minutes until completely smooth.

For Whole Chia Seed Version: Blend all ingredients except chia seeds in a blender until smooth (including any added flavors, fruits, or chocolate). After everything is blended, whisk in the chia seeds.

Pour mixture into a jar or glass container and place in the refrigerator for at least 4 hours or overnight to let gel. Within the first hour, be sure to stir or whisk t fhe mixture a few times to help it gel evenly. I recommend making this at night to have ready for a quick breakfast the next day. It is also great to make in the morning for a delicious pre-made dessert at night.

CINNAMON KETO GRANOLA

Ingredients

5 tbsp ground flax meal

5 tbsp unsweetened coconut flakes

1 tbsp Chia Seeds

1.5 oz nuts (we used pecans, walnuts and almonds)

4 tbsp sugar free maple syrup

1 1/2 tsp Cinnamon Optional

Directions

Thoroughly combine all ingredients except for the cinnamon.

Spread mixture onto a baking sheet, making one even layer.

Sprinkle cinnamon on top.

Bake at 350 degrees for 20-22 minutes.

Let rest. Granola will harden as it cools. Enjoy!

CINNAMON FRENCH TOFU STICKS WITH CHOCOLATE SYRUP

Ingredients

1 block extra firm tofu

4 tbsp Lakanto Monk Fruit Sweetener

1 tbsp cinnamon

For the chocolate syrup:

1/2 tbsp meted coconut oil

1 tbsp cacao or cocoa powder

Lakanto Maple-Flavored Syrup to taste

Directions

1. Drain tofu and wrap it in paper towels for 10-15 minutes.

2. While the tofu is draining, combine cinnamon and Lakanto in a mixing bowl for the cinnamon-sugar topping.

3. When the tofu is done draining, cut into uniform sticks and sprinkle with 1/4 of the cinnamon-sugar

topping.

4. Spray frypan with cooking spray on low heat. Place the tofu in pan.

5. Flip tofu every 3-4 minutes for about 30 minutes or until it is firm to the touch. Sprinkle tofu with more of the cinnamon-sugar topping after each flip until you've used all of the topping.

6. When the tofu is finished, prepare chocolate syrup.

7. Heat coconut oil in microwave for 30 seconds or until it liquifies.

8. Add cacao powder and liquid stevia to the coconut oil and mix thoroughly.

9. Drizzle chocolate syrup over the tofu sticks.

VEGAN KETO SANDWICH BREAD

Ingredients

160 g chia seeds

2 1/4 tsp instant yeast or one packet

800 mL warm water

100 g tahini or almond butter

100 g psyllium husks

10 g xanthan gum or guar gum

300 g almond flour

2 tsp salt

vegan keto bread 2

Directions

Mix the tahini and water together followed by the yeast and chia. Let sit for 20 mins or so until the chia is ready.

Mix the almond flour, psyllium husks, and gum with the salt.

When the chia mix is nice and goopy, mix it into your

dry ingredients, kneeding it until it comes together. Grease or line you bread tin with some parchment.

Add dough to tin and let rise in a warm place for at least an hour.

Bake in a 325 degrees oven for 90-120 mins until the internal temp reaches 200 degrees.

BASIC VEGAN FRENCH TOAST

Ingredients

1 heaping Tbsp chia seeds (whole or ground into a fine meal so that they're undetectable)

1/2 Tbsp agave nectar or maple syrup

1 cup unsweetened almond milk (or any non-dairy milk)

1/2 tsp ground cinnamon

1/2 tsp vanilla extract

4-5 bread slices (it's important to use a sturdy, rustic bread or it can turn out soggy/soft)

Directions

Mix all ingredients except the bread in a large, shallow bowl. Place in the fridge to marinade for 10-20 minutes.

Preheat griddle to medium heat (~350 degrees F / 176 C) and grease with 1 tbsp vegan butter or coconut oil.

Dip each slice of bread in the batter for about 20 seconds on each side. If your bread is dry, leave it in a little longer. Similarly, if you're using sandwich bread, it should only need 25-30 seconds total to soak.

Cook on a griddle until golden brown on the underside. Carefully flip and cook until the other side is golden brown as well, about 3-4 minutes.

Top with desired toppings such as coconut whipped cream, strawberries, and maple syrup.

VEGAN FRENCH TOAST

Ingredients

6 slices bread

1 cup non-dairy milk

2 tbsp silken tofu

1 tbsp nutritional yeast

1 tbsp sucanat or brown sugar

1 tsp vanilla

1/2 tsp sea salt

1/2 tsp cinnamon

dash of nutmeg

Directions

Put all ingredients except for the bread into a blender and blend until smooth. Preheat a skillet with oil, making sure to use a non-stick pan.

Dip the bread slices into the blended mixture and then place onto the skillet. Cook on both sides until browned. Serve with fruit and pure maple syrup if desired. Serves 2-3.

GLUTEN FREE VEGAN KETO BAGELS

Ingredients

3 tbsp flax seeds I used golden

1/2 cup tahini

1/4 cup psyllium powder

1/4 cup almond flour

1 tsp baking powder

1 cup water

Directions

Grind the flax seeds and add to psyllium, almond flour, and baking powder. You can choose to add salt here too if desired.

Mix water and tahini until smooth and then add to dry mix. Then, mix well until it is all combined, forming a dough ball.

Break into four pieces and shape into buns. You can either stick your finger though to make a hole like I do, or you can use a cutter.

Bake at 375 degrees for 45 mins.

When you're ready to serve, cut in half and re-toast for best texture.

AVOCADO SPREAD

Ingredients

2 medium ripe avocados

2 Tbsp fresh coriander leaves (finely chopped)

1 Tbsp fresh parsley leaves (finely chopped)

1/2 Tbsp fresh mint leaves (finely chopped)

1 garlic clove (crushed)

1/4 tsp ground cumin

juice of 1 to 2 lemons

1 roasted pepper (from a jar) finely chopped

sprinkle sunflower seeds

salt& pepper

Directions

Halve the avocados, scoop them out, and mash with a fork.

Add crushed garlic, ground cumin, chopped herbs, lemon juice, and roasted peppers.

Mixed together. Season to taste.

Spread on your favourite bread or bagel and sprinkle with sunflower seeds.

HOMEMADE SAMBAL

Ingredients

1 large onion

0.35 ounces dried birds-eye chilis

3 tbsp reduced sugar ketchup

2 tbsp coconut oil

1/2 tsp salt (or to taste)

Optional: 1-2 drops liquid sucralose

Directions

Chop onion and blend until smooth. Set aside.

Cut dried chilis and remove seeds. Boil them for about 30 minutes or until they are soft. Once soft and cooled, blend them to form a paste.

In a heated pan, melt coconut oil. Once hot, add the remaining ingredients. Optional: add in 1-2 drops Liquid Sucralose.

VEGAN SESAME TOFU AND EGGPLANT

Ingredients

1 pound block of firm tofu

1 cup (31g) chopped cilantro

3 tbsp rice vinegar

4 tbsp toasted sesame oil

2 cloves garlic, finely minced

1 tsp crushed red pepper flakes

2 tsps Swerve confectioners

1 whole (458 g) eggplant

1 tbsp olive oil

Salt and pepper to taste

1/4 cup sesame seeds

1/4 cup soy sauce

Directions

Preheat oven to 200°F. Remove the tofu from it's packaging and wrap it with paper towels. Place a plate on top to weigh it down. I used a large tin of vegetables in this picture, but you can use anything handy. Let the tofu sit for a while to press some of the water out.

Place about 1/4 cup of cilantro, 3 tbsp rice vinegar, 2 tbsp toasted sesame oil, minced garlic, crushed red pepper flakes, and transfer to a large mixing bowl. Whisk everything together.

Peel and julienne the eggplant. You can julienne roughly by hand like I did, or you can use a mandolin with a julienne attachment for more precise "noodles." Place the eggplant into the marinade.

Add olive oil to a skillet over medium-low heat and cook the eggplant until it softens. Keep in mind that the eggplant absorbs liquid, so if you have issues with it sticking to the pan, feel free to add a little bit more sesame or olive oil - just be sure to adjust your nutrition tracking.

Turn the oven off. Combine the remaining cilantro with the eggplant and transfer the noodles to an oven safe dish. Cover with a lid or foil, and place into the oven to keep warm. Clean out the skillet and return to the stovetop to heat up again.

Unwrap the tofu and cut it into 8 even slices. Spread the sesame seeds on a plate. Press both sides of each piece of tofu into the seeds to act as a crust.

Add 2 tbsps of sesame oil to the skillet. Fry both sides of the tofu for 5 minutes each, or until they start to crisp up. Pour the 1/4 cup of soy sauce into the pan and coat the pieces of tofu. Cook until the tofu slices look browned and caramelized with the soy sauce.

Remove the noodles from the oven and top with tofu.

ZUCCHINI RIBBONS & AVOCADO WALNUT PESTO

Ingredients

Zucchini Ribbons

3 medium zucchini

1/2 tsp salt

Avocado Walnut Pesto

1/2 large avocado

1 cup fresh basil leaves

1/4 cup walnuts

2 cloves garlic, peeled

1/2 large lemon

1/4 cup grated Parmesan cheese

1/2 cup water, if needed*

Other

1 tbsp olive oil

5-6 fresh basil leaves to garnish

Salt and pepper to taste

Directions

Cut the zucchini into delicate ribbons with a vegetable peeler or mandolin slicer, being careful to stop peeling once you reach the seeds.

Place the ribbons in a colander and toss with salt. Let stand while you prepare the avocado pesto.

Gather the avocado walnut pesto ingredients.

Add all ingredients into a food processor and blend until the sauce is smooth. If your sauce is too thick, you can add water to thin it as needed.

Grease a skillet with 1 tbsp olive oil and bring to medium heat.

Saute zucchini ribbons for 3-5 minutes or until they just begin to soften. Remove from heat.

Spoon pesto onto zucchini ribbons and gently toss to coat.

Plate two portions of fantastically swirled vegetable ribbons and garnish with fresh basil and grated Parmesan cheese.

LOW CARB FRIED MAC & CHEESE

Ingredients

1 medium cauliflower, riced

1 1/2 cups shredded cheddar cheese

3 large eggs

2 tsps paprika

1 tsp turmeric

3/4 tsp rosemary

Directions

Rice the cauliflower in a food processor then cook it in the microwave for 5 minutes.

Dry it out by wringing it in a kitchen towel or paper towels; you want as little moisture as possible.

Add your eggs one by one followed by cheese and spices to the cauliflower and mix together.

Heat olive oil and coconut oil in a pan on high heat.

Form small patties out of the cauliflower mixture.

Fry on both sides until crisp.

TOMATO BASIL AND MOZZARELLA GALETTE

Ingredients

1 cup almond flour

1 large egg

3 tbsp mozzarella liquid

1 tsp garlic powder

1/4 cup shredded Parmesan cheese

2 tbsp pesto

3-4 fresh basil leaves

1/2 ounce Mozzarella pearls*

3-4 cherry tomatoes

Directions

Heat oven to 375°F and line a cookie sheet with parchment, spraying it with non stick spray. Combine the almond flour, garlic powder, and mozzarella liquid in a bowl, stirring gently.

Add the egg and Parmesan cheese, then mix well until dough forms.

Form the dough mixture into a large ball and place on the prepared parchment.

Press the dough ball into a circle, working to keep the thickness uniform. It should press out to about 1/2 inch thick. It may be sticky, so wetting your hands with water can help keep your fingers from sticking to the crust.

Spread pesto evenly over the center of the crust, leaving room to fold in the edges. Layer mozzarella, basil leaves, and tomatoes.

Using the edge of the parchment, fold the edges of the crust up and over the filling. Work in a circle around the edge until all of the edges are folded up.

Bake for 20 to 25 minutes or until the crust is golden brown and the cheese is melted.

KETO GRILLED CHEESE SANDWICH

Ingredients

Bun Ingredients

2 large eggs

2 tbsp almond flour

1 1/2 tbsps psyllium husk powder

1/2 tsp baking powder

2 tbsp butter, softened

Fillings & Extras

2 ounces cheddar cheese

1 tbsp butter

Directions

Mix all of the bun ingredients together in a bowl and mix until it thickens up.

Pour mixture into a square bowl or container and level it off. Clean sides if needed.

Microwave for 90 seconds. If more time is needed, continue cooking in 15 second intervals.

Once cooked, remove bread from container and slice in half.

Put cheese between bun, heat butter in a pan over medium heat, and fry the grilled cheese until you are happy with the texture.

FRESH BELL PEPPER BASIL PIZZA

Ingredients

Pizza Base

6 ounces mozzarella cheese

1/2 cup almond flour

2 tbsp psyllium husk

2 tbsps cream cheese

2 tbsps fresh Parmesan cheese

1 large egg

1 tsp Italian seasoning

1/2 tsp salt

1/2 tsp pepper

Toppings

4 ounces shredded cheddar cheese

1 medium vine tomato

1/4 cup Rao's Marinara Sauce

2/3 medium bell pepper

2-3 tbsp fresh chopped basil

Directions

1. Preheat oven to 400F.

2. Microwave mozarella cheese for 40-50 seconds or until completely melted and pliable.

3. Add the rest of the pizza ingredients (EXCEPT for toppings) to the cheese and mix together well. I recommend using your hands.

4. Using your hands or a rolling pin, flatten the dough and form a circle.

5. Bake for 10 minutes and remove pizza from the oven. Top the pizza with the toppings and bake for another 8-10 minutes.

6. Remove pizza from the oven and let cool.

KETO BREAKFAST BROWNIE MUFFINS

Ingredients

1 cup golden flaxseed meal

1/4 cup cocoa powder

1 tbsp cinnamon

1/2 tbsp baking powder

1/2 tsp salt

1 large egg

2 tbsp coconut oil

1/4 cup sugar-free caramel syrup

1/2 cup pumpkin puree

1 tsp vanilla extract

1 tsp apple cider vinegar

1/4 cup slivered almonds

Directions

Preheat your oven to 350°F and combine all ingredients in a deep mixing bowl and mix to combine.

Line a muffin tin with 6 paper liners and spoon about 1/4 cup of batter into each muffin liner.

Sprinkle slivered almonds over the top of each muffin and press gently so that they stay.

Bake in the oven for about 15 minutes. You should see the muffins rise and set on top.

VEGETARIAN GREEK COLLARD WRAPS

Ingredients

Tzatziki Sauce

1 cup plain Greek yogurt, full-fat

1 tsp garlic powder

1 tbsp white vinegar

2 tbsp olive oil

2.5 ounces (1/4) cucumber, seeded and grated

2 tbsp minced fresh dill

Salt and pepper to taste

The Wrap

4 large collard green leaves, washed

1 medium cucumber, julienned

1/2 medium red bell pepper, julienned

1/2 cup purple onion, diced

8 kalamata olives, halved

1/2 block (4-oz) feta, cut into 4 (1-inch thick) strips

4 cherry tomatoes, halved

Directions

Mix all of the ingredients for the tzatziki sauce together then store it in the fridge. Be sure to squeeze all of the water out of the cucumber after you grate it.

Prepare collard green wraps by washing leaves well and trimming the fibrous stem from each leaf.

Spread 2 tbsp of tzatziki onto the center of each wrap and smooth the sauce out.

Layer the cucumber, pepper, onion, olives, feta, and tomatoes in the center of the wrap. I've shown them spread out in a line to display each ingredient, but when assembling these wraps, it works best to keep all of the ingredients close and toward the center of the leaf. Imagine piling them high rather than spreading them out!

Fold as you would a burrito, folding in each side toward the center and the folding the rounded end over the filling and roll.

You can slice the wraps in half and serve with any leftover tzatziki or save it as a leftover meal!

SUN DRIED TOMATO PESTO MUG CAKE

Ingredients

Base

1 large egg

2 tbsps butter

2 tbsp almond flour

1/2 tsp baking powder

Flavor

5 tsps sun dried tomato pesto

1 tbsp almond flour

Pinch salt

Directions

Mix all ingredients together.

Microwave for 75 seconds on high (power level 10).

You can either lightly tap the cup against plate to take the mug cake out or you can take a butter knife around the edges of the cake to loosen it. Add extra tomato pesto and serve!

SESAME ALMOND ZOODLE BOWL

Ingredients

Zoodles

2 medium zucchini, spiralized

1/2 cup sliced mushrooms

1 cup shredded broccoli slaw*

1 tsp sesame oil

Sauce

1/4 cup almond butter

2 tbsp soy sauce

2 tbsp sesame oil

1/4 tsp garlic powder

1 tsp crushed red pepper flakes

1 tsp erythritol

2 tbsp chopped almonds, garnish

Optional: Pinch of chili powder

Directions

Heat 1 tsp of sesame oil in a large skillet on medium heat. Add the shredded broccoli and cabbage mix along with the mushrooms and sauté until they begin to soften.

Make your zucchini noodles using a vegetable spiralizer and pat them dry with a towel to remove some of the excess moisture.

Add your zoodles to the skillet and heat evenly by gently turning the zoodles with a fork or tongs until the noodles become soft but not soggy, about 3-5 minutes.

Make your sauce by adding all ingredients in a large bowl and combining thoroughly.

Add a touch more water or oil if necessary to reach your desired consistency.

Portion your zoodles in three bowls and drizzle with sesame almond sauce then toss to coat.

Top with chopped almonds and crushed red pepper flakes and an optional pinch of chili powder.

CHEESY THYME WAFFLES

Ingredients

1/2 large head cauliflower, riced

1 cup finely shredded mozzarella cheese

1 cup packed collard greens

1/3 cup Parmesan cheese

2 large eggs

2 stalks green onion

1 tbsp sesame seed

1 tbsp olive oil

2 tsps fresh chopped thyme

1 tsp garlic powder

1/2 tsp ground black pepper

1/2 tsp salt

Directions

Rice the cauliflower by pulsing the florets in a food processor until a crumbly texture is achieved.

Add collard greens, spring onion, and thyme, then continue pulsing until everything is well combined.

Scoop the mixture out into a mixing bowl, add the rest of the ingredients, and mix together well.

Spoon mixture evenly over the griddle of a waffle iron once it's hot.

Cook the waffle according to your waffle makers' manufacturing instructions, then remove.

CHEESY HEARTS OF PALM DIP

Ingredients

1 (14-ounce) can hearts of palm, drained

3 green onions stalks, chopped

1/4 cup mayonnaise

2 tbsp Italian seasoning

1/2 cup Parmesan cheese, shredded

2 large eggs, separate 1 of the eggs

Topping

1/4 cup Parmesan cheese

Directions

Heat oven to 350°F and prepare a small baking dish with nonstick spray.

Chop the green onion bulbs and drain your hearts of palm. It is not necessary to cut the palm before adding it to your food processor, but it can help if you have an older or less powerful model.

Combine the Hearts of Palm, onion, seasoning, Parmesan cheese, and mayo in the food processor. Pulse until the mixture is smooth.

Add one whole egg and one egg yolk to the processor. Pulse three to four times to combine.

Pour the dip into prepared baking dish and cook for 15 – 20 minutes or until the mixture begins to puff up slightly. Stir and top with more Parmesan cheese.

Broil until the cheese is melted and begins to brown. Serve hot with veggies or keto crackers.

LOW CARB BROCCOLI AND CHEESE FRITTERS

Ingredients

Fritters

3/4 cup almond flour

1/4 cup + 3 tbsp flaxseed meal

4 ounces fresh broccoli

4 ounces mozzarella cheese

2 large eggs

2 tsps baking powder

Salt and Pepper to taste

Sauce

1/4 cup mayonnaise

1/4 cup fresh chopped dill

1/2 tbsp lemon juice

Salt and pepper to taste

Directions

Add broccoli to a food processor and process until broccoli is completely broken down.

Add cheese, almond flour, 1/4 cup flaxseed meal, and baking powder. If you want to add any extra seasonings (salt and pepper), so at this point.

Add the eggs and mix together well until everything is incorperated.

Roll the batter into balls and then coat with 3 tbsp flaxseed meal.

Heat your deep fryer to 375F and lay fritters inside the basket, not overcrowing it.

Fry the fritters until they are golden brown, about 3-5 minutes. Once done, lay them on paper towels to drain excess grease and season to your tastes.

If desired, you can make a zesty dill and lemon mayonnaise for a dip. Enjoy!

WARM ASIAN BROCCOLI SALAD

Ingredients

12 ounce bag broccoli slaw

2 tbsps coconut oil

1 tbsp coconut aminos

1 tsp fresh ginger, grated

1/2 tsp salt

1/4 tsp pepper

1/2 cup full fat plain goat milk yogurt

1/2 tbsp sesame seeds

Cilantro, as an optional garnish

Directions

Preheat coconut oil in a large skillet over medium high heat. Place the broccoli slaw into the skillet, cover, and cook for 7 minutes.

Remove the lid fro the skillet and stir in the coconut aminos, ginger, salt and pepper. Remove your skillet from the heat, then stir in yogurt and top with sesame seeds.

Garnish with cilantro, if desired.

CAULIFLOWER MAC & CHEESE

Ingredients

2 pounds frozen cauliflower florets

1 cup heavy whipping cream

4 ounces cream cheese, cubed

8 ounces cheddar cheese, shredded

1 tsps Dijon mustard

1 tsp turmeric

1/2 tsp powdered garlic

Salt and pepper to taste

Directions

Cook the cauliflower florets according to the package instructions.

Bring the cream to a simmer. Then, use a whisk to stir in the cream cheese and mix until smooth.

Stir in 6 ounces of the shredded cheddar cheese, saving the other 2 ounces for later. Mix until the cheese melts into the sauce.

Add the Dijon mustard, turmeric, powdered garlic, salt, and pepper. The sauce will become a smooth yellow color.

Make sure that the cauliflower is drained, then add it to the cheese sauce. Evenly coat the florets with sauce.

Sprinkle on the remaining 2 ounces of cheddar cheese, then stir until mostly melted.

PERSONAL PAN PIZZA DIP

Ingredients

Personal Pan Pizza Dip

4 ounces cream cheese

1/4 cup sour cream

1/4 cup mayonnaise

1 cup shredded mozzarella cheese

Salt and pepper to taste

1/2 cup Rao's tomato sauce

1/4 cup Parmesan cheese

Pepperoni, Peppers, and Olives

6 slices pepperoni, chopped

1 tbsp diced green pepper

4 pitted sliced black olives

1/2 tsp Italian seasoning

Salt and pepper to taste

Mushrooms and Peppers

1 tbsp diced green pepper

2 tbsp diced baby bella mushrooms

1/2 tsp Italian seasoning

Salt and pepper to taste

Directions

Pre-heat oven to 350F. Measure out the cream cheese and microwave for 20 seconds or leave it out until it is room temperature.

Mix the sour cream, mayonnaise, and mozzarella cheese into the cream cheese. Season with salt and pepper to taste.

Divide the mixture between 4 ramekins, then spoon 2 tbsp of tomato sauce over each ramekin.

Measure out 1/2 cup mozzarella cheese and 1/4 cup parmesan cheese, then sprinkle mixture over the the sauce evenly.

Add toppings of choice to your personal pan pizza dips.

Bake for 18-20 minutes or until cheese is bubbling.

Remove from oven and let cool.

VEGETARIAN THREE CHEESE QUICHE STUFFED PEPPERS

Ingredients

2 medium bell peppers, halved and seeded

4 large eggs

1/2 cup ricotta cheese

1/2 cup shredded mozzarella

1/2 cup grated Parmesan cheese

1 tsp garlic powder

1/4 tsp dried parsley

1/4 cup baby spinach leaves

2 tbsp Parmesan cheese, to garnish

Directions

Heat oven to 375°F. Prepare the peppers by slicing them into four equal halves and removing the seeds.

In a small food processor, blend the three cheeses, eggs, garlic powder, and parsley. My food processor is smaller than I would like, so I did this in two batches, half and half, and then combined both fillings.

Pour the egg mixture into each pepper, filling just below the rim. Place a few baby spinach leaves on top and stir with a fork, pushing them under the egg.

Cover with foil and bake for 35-45 minutes or until the egg is set.

Sprinkle with Parmesan cheese and broil for 3-5 minutes or until the tops begin to brown.

ROASTED MUSHROOM AND WALNUT CAULIFLOWER GRITS

Ingredients

6 ounces baby portobello mushrooms, sliced

3 cloves garlic, minced

1 tbsp rosemary

1/2 cup chopped walnuts

1 tbsp smoked paprika

2 tbsp olive oil

1 medium head of cauliflower

1/2 cup water

1 cup half-and-half

1 cup shredded sharp cheddar

2 tbsp butter

Salt to taste

Directions

Heat oven to 400°F and line a cookie sheet with foil. Combine the sliced mushrooms, minced garlic, rosemary, walnuts, and smoked paprika in a small dish and drizzle with olive oil. Toss to coat and season with salt.

Spread the mixture evenly on the cookie sheet and roast in the oven for 15 minutes.

Process one head of cauliflower florets in a food processor by pulsing it until it is very fine.

Steam the processed cauliflower in a medium pot, covered, with 1/2 cup water for 5 minutes or until the mixture is slightly tender. You don't want it to be too soft since it will need to resemble grits.

Pour half-and-half into the cauliflower grits, stir, and simmer on medium-low heat for 3 minutes or just until the milk is heated.

Stir in the sharp cheddar and butter and reduce heat to low until the mixture is creamy and well combined. Season with salt to taste. If you like your grits runny add another 1/4 cup of water.

Remove roasting pan from the oven once the mushrooms are soft and the edges are a deep brown.

Serve the cauliflower grits hot, and top with the mushroom mixture and extra butter if desired.

CHARRED VEGGIE AND FRIED GOAT CHEESE SALAD

Ingredients

2 tbsp poppy seeds

2 tbsp sesame seeds

1 tsp onion flakes

1 tsp garlic flakes

4 ounces goat cheese, cut into 4 1/2 in thick medallions

1 medium red bell pepper, seeds removed & cut into 8 pieces

1/2 cup baby portobello mushrooms, sliced

4 cups arugula, divided between two bowls

1 tbsp avocado oil

Directions

1. Combine the poppy and sesame seeds, onion, and garlic flakes in a small dish.

2. Coat each piece of goat cheese on both sides then plate and place in the refrigerator until you are ready to fry the cheese.

3. Prepare a skillet with nonstick spray and bring to medium heat. Char the peppers and mushrooms on both sides, just until the pieces begin to darken and the pepper softens. Add to the bowls of arugula.

4. Place the cold goat cheese in the skillet and fry on each side for about 30 seconds. This melts quickly so be gentle as you flip each piece!

5. Add the cheese to the salad and drizzle with avocado oil. Serve warm!

CRISPY TOFU AND BOK CHOY SALAD

Ingredients

15 ounces extra firm tofu

1 tbsp soy sauce

1 tbsp sesame oil

1 tbsp water

2 tsps minced garlic

1 tbsp rice wine vinegar

Juice of 1/2 lemon

Bok Choy Salad

9 ounces bok choy

1 stalk green onion

2 tbsp chopped cilantro

3 tbsp coconut oil

2 tbsp soy sauce

1 tbsp sambal olek

1 tbsp peanut butter

Juice 1/2 lime

7 drops liquid stevia

Directions

1. Start by pressing the tofu by placing it in a kitchen towel with something heavy over the top (like a cast iron skillet). This is a long process as it takes about 4-6 hours to dry out. Additionally, you may need to replace the kitchen towel half-way through.

2. Once the tofu is pressed, start your marinade by combining all of the ingredients for the marinade (soy sauce, sesame oil, water, garlic, vinegar, and lemon).

3. Chop the tofu into squares and place in a plastic bag along with the marinade. Let this marinate for at least 30 minutes, but preferably over night.

4. Pre-heat oven to 350°F. Place tofu on a baking sheet lined with parchment paper (or a silpat) and bake for 30-35 minutes.

5. As the tofu cooks, get started on the bok choy salad by chopping cilantro and spring onion.

6. Mix all of the other ingredients together (except lime juice and bok choy) in a bowl. Then add cilantro and spring onion.

Note: You can microwave coconut oil for 10-15 seconds to allow it it to melt.

7. Once the tofu is almost cooked, add lime juice into the salad dressing and mix together.

8. Chop the bok choy into small slices, like you would cabbage.

9. Remove the tofu from the oven and assemble your salad with tofu, bok choy, and sauce.

VEGETARIAN GREEK COLLARD WRAPS

Ingredients

Tzatziki Sauce

1 cup plain Greek yogurt, full-fat

1 tsp garlic powder

1 tbsp white vinegar

2 tbsp olive oil

2.5 ounces (1/4) cucumber, seeded and grated

2 tbsps minced fresh dill

Salt and pepper to taste

The Wrap

4 large collard green leaves, washed

1 medium cucumber, julienned

1/2 medium red bell pepper, julienned

1/2 cup purple onion, diced

8 kalamata olives, halved

1/2 block (4-oz) feta, cut into 4 (1-inch thick) strips

4 cherry tomatoes, halved

Directions

Mix all of the ingredients for the tzatziki sauce together and store it in the fridge.

Note: Be sure to squeeze all of the water out of the cucumber after you grate it.

Prepare collard green wraps by washing the leaves well and trimming the fibrous stem from each leaf.

Spread 2 tbsps of tzatziki onto the center of each wrap and smooth the sauce out.

Layer the cucumber, peppers, onion, olives, feta, and tomatoes in the center of the wrap. I've shown them spread out in a line to display each ingredient, but when assembling these wraps, it actually works best to keep all of the ingredients close and toward the center of the leaf. Imagine piling them high rather than spreading them out!

Fold the wrap the same way that you fold a burrito, brinigng in each side toward the center and the folding the rounded end over the filling and roll.

Slice in half and serve with any leftover tzatziki or wrap in plastic for easy leftovers.

Notes

Nutrition breakdown accounts for approximately 2 tbsp of tzatziki per wrap.

SESAME ALMOND ZOODLE BOWL

Ingredients

Zoodles

    2 medium zucchini, spiralized

    1/2 cup sliced mushrooms

    1 cup shredded broccoli slaw

    1 tsp sesame oil

Sauce

    1/4 cup almond butter

    2 tbsp soy sauce

    2 tbsp sesame oil

    1/4 tsp garlic powder

    1 tsp crushed red pepper flakes

    1 tsp erythritol

    2 tbsp chopped almonds, garnish

Optional: pinch of chili powder

Directions

1. Heat 1 tsp of sesame oil in a large skillet on medium heat. Add the shredded broccoli cabbage mix and mushrooms, then sauté until they begin to soften.

2. Make your zucchini noodles using a vegetable spiralizer and pat them dry with a towel to remove excess moisture.

3. Add your zoodles to the skillet and heat evenly by gently turning the zoodles with a fork or tongs until the noodles become soft but not soggy, about 3-5 minutes.

4. Mix your sauce by adding all ingredients in a large bowl and combining thoroughly.

 5. If you desire a thinner consistency, you ca nadd more water or oil.

6. Portion your zoodles in three bowls and drizzle with sesame almond sauce then toss to coat.

7. Top with chopped almonds and crushed red pepper flakes and an optional pinch of chili powder.

VEGETARIAN THREE CHEESE QUICHE STUFFED PEPPERS

Ingredients

2 medium bell peppers, sliced in half and seeded

4 large eggs

1/2 cup ricotta cheese

1/2 cup shredded mozzarella

1/2 cup grated Parmesan cheese

1 tsp garlic powder

1/4 tsp dried parsley

1/4 cup baby spinach leaves

2 tbsps Parmesan cheese, to garnish

Directions

1. Heat oven to 375°F. Prepare the peppers by slicing them each into equal halves. Remove the seeds.

2. In a small food processor, blend the three cheeses, eggs, garlic powder, and parsley. My food processor is smaller than I would like so I did this in two batches, half and half, and then combined both fillings.

3. Pour the egg mixture into each pepper, filling just below the rim. Place baby spinach leaves on top and stir with a fork, pushing them under the egg. Cover with foil and bake for 35-45 minutes or until the egg is set.

4. Sprinkle with Parmesan cheese and broil for 3-5 minutes or until the tops begin to brown

VEGETARIAN RED COCONUT CURRY

Ingredients

1 cup broccoli florets

1 large handful of spinach

4 tbsp coconut oil

1/4 medium onion

1 tsp minced garlic

1 tsp minced ginger

2 tsps Fish sauce

2 tsps soy sauce

1 tbsp red curry paste

1/2 cup coconut cream (or coconut milk)

Directions

Chop onions and minced garlic. Add 2 tbsp of coconut oil to a pan and bring it to medium-high heat.

Once hot, add the onions to the pan and cook until they are semi-translucent. Then, add garlic to the the pan until fragrant.

Turn heat down to medium-low and add broccoli to the pan, stirring everything well together.

Once broccoli is partially cooked, move vegetables to the side of the pan and add curry paste. Let this cook for 45-60 seconds.

Add spinach and once it begins to wilt, add the coconut cream along with the rest of the coconut oil.

Stir together and add soy sauce, fish sauce, and ginger. Let simmer for 5-10 minutes or until the sauce reaches your desired consistency.

VEGAN KETO PORRIDGE

Ingredients

2 tbsp coconut flour

3 tbsp golden flaxseed meal

2 tbsps vegan vanilla protein powder*

1 1/2 cups unsweetened almond milk

Powdered erythritol to taste

Note: Try experimenting with different flavors!

Directions

1. In a bowl, mix together the coconut flour, golden flaxseed meal, and protein powder.

2. Add to a sauce pan along with the almond milk and cook over medium heat.

3. It will seem very loose at first, but when it thickens, you can stir in your preferred amount of sweetener. I like to use about 1/2 a tbsp. Serve with your favorite toppings.

LEMON RASPBERRY SWEET ROLLS

Ingredients

Lemon cream cheese filling

4 oz cream cheese, room temperature

2 tbsp butter, room temperature

2 tbsp stevia erythritol blend*

1/2 tsp vanilla extract

1 tsp lemon extract

Zest from one lemon (about 2 tsps)

1 tsp Lemon juice

Raspberry sauce:

2 tbsp stevia erythritol blend*

1/4 tsp xanthan gum

1 tbsp water

2 tsps lemon juice

1/2 cup frozen raspberries

Dough:

1 cup super fine almond flour

1/4 cup stevia erythritol blend*

1/4 tsp zanthan gum

1 1/4 tsp baking powder

1 large egg

1 tsp vanilla extract

2 cups part-skim mozzarella cheese

Lemon glaze (optional)

2 tbsp butter, room temperature

1/2 ounce cream cheese, room temperature

1/4 tsp vanilla extract

2 tbsp stevia erythritol blend*

1 tsp lemon juice

1/4 tsp lemon extract

1 1/2 tbsp unsweetened almond milk, room temperature

Directions

Lemon Cream Cheese Filling:

Use an electric mixer to beat the cream cheese, butter, sweetener, vanilla extract, lemon extract, lemon zest, and lemon juice until smooth. Set aside.

Raspberry Sauce:

In a medium saucepan, whisk together sweetener and xanthan gum. Gradually add water and lemon juice while whisking.

Set heat to medium-low and add frozen raspberries, stirring constantly. Just when the sauce begins to simmer, remove from heat and set aside.

Dough:

Preheat oven to 350F degrees. Spray a 9" circular pan with coconut oil or grease with butter. Have two 15 inch sheets of parchment and a rolling pin handy.

Prepare a double boiler – a medium saucepan with a medium bowl that will sit on top works fine for this purpose. Add about 2 inches of water to the saucepan or the bottom part of the double boiler. Place over high heat and bring to a simmer uncovered. Once it begins to simmer, reduce heat to low.

Meanwhile in the top-part of the double boiler (with it not over the water), combine the almond flour, stevia/erythritol sweetener, xanthan gum, and baking powder using a whisk.

Stir in the egg and vanilla extract. Keep in mind that the mixture will be very thick.

Stir in the mozzarella cheese and place the bowl over the pot of simmering water. Be sure to protect your hands from the hot bowl and the steam escaping the pot (a silicone mitten works well for this purpose).

Stir the mixture constantly while the cheese melts and combines with the flour. It will begin to look like bread dough.

When the cheese has melted completely, transfer the dough to a prepared piece of parchment paper. Knead the dough until the flour is completely combined with with the cheese. Pat dough into a rectangular shape and cover with the second piece of parchment. Roll out dough into about 12" X 15" rectangle.

Remove top parchment.

Evenly spread the lemon cream cheese filling on the dough, leaving about 1/2 inch uncovered on the edges, then spread the raspberry sauce over the lemon cream cheese filling.

Starting at the long side, roll the dough into a log shape.Press the outside long edge to seal.

Using a serrated knife, gently cut the log crosswise

into 8 pieces. Arrange rolls in the prepared pan with one roll in the center and the rest circled around it.

Bake for 24-26 minutes, or until golden brown.

Lemon glaze:

In a small bowl, beat butter and cream cheese with an electric mixer until smooth.

Add vanilla, sweetener, lemon juice, and lemon extract until incorporated.

Gradually add the almond milk, one tsp at a time, beating the mixture between each addition.

KETO BREAKFAST BROWNIE MUFFINS

Ingredients

1 cup golden flaxseed meal

1/4 cup cocoa powder

1 tbsp cinnamon

1/2 tbsp baking powder

1/2 tsp salt

1 large egg

2 tbsp coconut oil

1/4 cup sugar-free caramel syrup

1/2 cup pumpkin puree

1 tsp vanilla extract

1 tsp apple cider vinegar

1/4 cup slivered almonds

Directions

1. Preheat your oven to 350°F and combine all your dry ingredients in a deep mixing bowl; mix to combine.

2. In a separate bowl, combine all your wet ingredients.

3. Combine you wet ingredients with your dry ingredients and mix well.

4. Line a muffin tin with paper liners and spoon about 1/4 cup of batter into each muffin liner. This recipe should yield 6 muffins. Sprinkle slivered almonds over the top of each muffin and press gently so that they stick.

5. Bake in the oven for about 15 minutes. You should see the muffins rise and set on top. Enjoy warm or cool.

AVOCADO CHOCOLATE MOUSSE

Ingredients

4 ounces chopped semisweet chocolate or chocolate chips (at least 60% dark), about 1/2 cup plus 2 tbsps

2 large, ripe avocados

3 tbsps unsweetened cocoa powder

1/4 cup Almond Breeze Unsweetened Almondmilk Cashewmilk Blend

1 tsp pure vanilla extract

1/8 tsp kosher salt

For serving: fresh raspberries, sliced strawberries, whipped cream (or whipped coconut cream to keep vegan), and chocolate shavings

Directions

Place the chopped chocolate or chocolate chips in a microwave-safe bowl. Microwave in 15-second increments, stirring between each and watching carefully so that the chocolate does not burn. When the chocolate is almost completely melted, remove it from the microwave and stir until smooth. Set aside and let cool until just barely warm.

Halve and pit the avocados, then scoop them into a food processor fitted with a steel blade. Add the melted chocolate, cocoa powder, almond milk/cashew milk blend, vanilla extract, and salt. Blend until very smooth and creamy, stopping to scrape down the bowl as needed. Taste and add a few teaspoons of agave if you would like it to be a bit sweeter. Spoon into glasses. Enjoy immediately as a pudding, or for a thicker, mousse-like consistency, refrigerate until well chilled, 2 hours or overnight. Serve topped with raspberries, cream, and chocolate shavings.

CAULIFLOWER SOUP

Ingredients

3 tsps olive oil

1 1/2 pounds cauliflower, roughly chopped

1 1/4 cups green cabbage, roughly chopped

1/2 cup leeks, roughly chopped

2 tbsp garlic, minced

1/2 cup parsnip, roughly chopped

1 1/2 tsps rosemary, minced

3/4 tsp thyme leaves

2 cups coconut milk

2 1/2 cups celery juice (or vegetable stock)

1 tsp Himalayan salt (additional to taste)

Black pepper, freshly cracked, to taste

Nutmeg, to taste

Directions

Heat the oil in the stock pot, and sauté the cauliflower, leeks, parsnips, garlic, rosemary, and thyme until the cauliflower is slightly browned.

Add the celery juice (or vegetable stock) and coconut milk and let it simmer for approximately 30 minutes. Season with salt, pepper, and nutmeg.

Blend until smooth, either using a handheld immersion blender or transferring your soup to a food processor or blender in 2 or 3 batches (depending on the size of the blender.)

CHEESY EGG MUFFINS

Ingredients

1 dozen eggs

1/2 tsp sea salt

Ghee or nonstick cooking spray, to coat pans

1 cup frozen or fresh spinach

1 heaping cup thinly sliced mushrooms

1/4 cup thinly sliced green onion

1 1/2 to 2 cups shredded cheese (either cheddar or parmesan)

Directions

Preheat the oven to 350°F. Crack eggs into a liquid measuring cup and whisk them with salt.

Grease a 12-cup muffin pan with butter or ghee. Divide spinach, mushrooms, green onion, and cheese between each muffin cup, then carefully pour eggs over tops until muffin tins are almost full (leave 1/4-inch of space).

Bake for 20-25 minutes or until a wooden pick, knife, etc. that is inserted in the center of a muffin comes out clean. The egg muffins will look like soufflé when they come out of the oven, but will sink after a few minutes. Let them rest in the muffin tin for a few minutes before carefully removing each muffin using a rubber spatula.

Serve immediately or let cool and transfer to a resealable plastic bag. Refrigerate for up to a week or freeze for a month.

ITALIAN BAKED EGG AND VEGETABLES

Ingredients

1 pound plum tomatoes, cut into 1-inch chunks

1 red bell pepper, cut into 3/4-inch pieces

1 zucchini, quartered lengthwise, cut crosswise into 3/4-inch chunks

1 onion, halved lengthwise, sliced

2 large garlic cloves, minced

1/2 tsp dried basil (or 1/2 tbsp fresh)

1/2 tsp salt

1/4 tsp black pepper

4 large eggs

1/4 cup grated fat-free parmesan cheese

Directions

Heat oven to 400°F, and cover a shallow roasting pan with nonstick cooking spray. Put the tomatoes, bell pepper, zucchini, onion, garlic, basil, salt, and pepper in pan and also spray with nonstick spray (or use olive oil). Toss to coat. Roast, stirring occasionally, until vegetables are browned and tender, about 30 minutes.

Spray four 8 or 10 ounce ramekins or custard cups with nonstick spray. Divide roasted vegetables evenly among cups. Make a well in the center of the vegetables, and carefully break one egg into each cup. Sprinkle with parmesan cheese. Place cups on baking sheet, and bake until eggs are just set, about 20 to 25 minutes.

KETO TABBOULEH

Ingredients

    1/2 cup (120 ml) extra-virgin olive oil

    1/4 cup (80 ml) lemon juice

    1/2 tsp gray sea salt

    2 bunches of fresh parsley, chopped

    1⅓ cup (215 g) Manitoba Harvest Hemp Hearts

    3 medium tomatoes, diced

    8 green onions, finely diced

    1/4 cup (24 g) chopped fresh mint

    1 small garlic clove, minced

Directions

Place the olive oil, lemon juice and sea salt in a large bowl, Whisk to combine.

Add remaining ingredients and toss to coat. Serve

VEGAN KETO COOKIE CARAMEL COOKIE BARS

Ingredients

1/2 cup (112g) coconut oil, softened

1/2 cup unsweetened coconut milk or preferred non-dairy milk

2 tbsp (10g) whole psyllium husk

2 tbsp (24g) golden granulated sweetener

1/4 tsp salt

1 tsp vanilla extract

1/2 cup (50g) coconut flour

1/2 cup (30g) unsweetened coconut flakes

1/2 cup (56g) raw macadamia nut halves

1 ounce (30g) unsweetened baking chocolate

1/4 cup (60ml) Coconut Dulce de Leche

Directions

Preheat the oven to 350°F (177°C) and line an 8"x8" (20cm x 20cm) brownie pan with parchment paper, leaving at least 2" (5cm) extra on two opposing sides to make it easier to remove them from the pan.

In a medium mixing bowl, mix the coconut oil, coconut milk, psyllium, granulated sweetener, salt and vanilla until completely combined and smooth. This takes about a minute of stirring.

Next, add the coconut flour, coconut flakes, macadamia nuts and chocolate and stir until everything is evenly distributed. The dough will resemble a drop cookie dough batter.

Press the dough evenly into the brownie pan and bake for 30 minutes or until the peaks begin to turn golden and the dough is firm to the touch.

Remove from the pan using the extra parchment as handles and let cool for an hour so the bars have time to set up. You can also speed this process up by putting the bars in the freezer for about 15 minutes .

Once cooled, slice into 9 equal portions and either drizzle or pipe the Quick Coconut Dulce de Leche on top.

To store the bars, refrigerate them in a covered container for up to four days or freeze for up to a month.

KETO COCONUT DULCE DE LECHE

Ingredients

2 cans (13.5oz/400ml each) coconut milk, full fat

1/4 cup, plus 1 tbsp (60g) granulated sweetener

1/4 tsp saltu8

Directions

In a large saucepan on medium-high heat, stir ingredients together. Heat for about five minutes, whisking occasionally until the mixture begins to boil.

Turn the heat down to medium and continue whisking frequently making sure that you whisk away the "foam" that appears. Once this foam is completely gone (about 13-14 minutes), cook for another minute, whisking constantly. This will bring the cooking time to about 20 minutes total.

The dulce de leche will have thickened to a caramel consistency and will be a medium golden color.

Let it cool for about ten minutes before either using or transferring to a heat-safe jar and continuing to cool, uncovered, in the fridge. Once cool, cover and store.

To store, refrigerate in a sealed jar for up to two weeks.

To reheat, scoop the caramel into a small saucepan on low heat and gently heat for about five minutes, whisking occasionally, until the caramel becomes smooth and pourable.

VEGAN KETO MAPLE CINNAMON NOATMEAL

Ingredients

3 tbsp (30g) hulled hemp seeds

3 tbsp (30g) Vega Clean Protein in vanilla

2 tbsp (15g) ground flax seeds

1/2 tsp ground cinnamon

2 tbsp Lakanto sugar-free maple syrup

3/4 cup (180ml) hot water

Directions

Stir dry ingredients together in a bowl. Next, pour the water over, and continue stirring until the lumps are gone. The mixture will continue to thicken as it cools.

Top with sugar-free maple syrup.

PANCAKE MUFFINS

Ingredients

1/2 cup plain yogurt, whole milk

2 tbsp coconut oil or unsalted butter, melted

1 tsp vanilla extract

1/4 tsp apple cider vinegar

1 3/4 cup almond flour

1/2 tsp baking soda

1 tsp salt

3 eggs

Directions

- Place muffin cups in your 6-12 space tray.

- Preheat oven to 350 degrees.

- Blend yogurt, oil, vinegar, extract, and any sweetener you have together. Add the flour, salt, and baking soda. Blend until combined.

- Now add in the eggs and blend again. Pop it on a high setting and blend for about 30 seconds until the eggs just mix in to create your batter.

- Now add in all your other ingredients and stir by hand.

- Place the batter into your muffin liners. Add some chopped walnuts or almonds on top if you wish.

- Bake for around 15-20 minutes. To test if they're done, stick a knife or toothpick into the middle and see if it comes out clean. If not, then the muffins need to go back in for a few more minutes, just be sure to watch them carefully.

POPPY SEED MUFFINS

Ingredients

3/4 cup almond flour

1/4 cup flaxseed meal

1/3 cup natural sweetener (Erythritol)

1tsp baking powder

1/4 cup unsalted butter

1/4 cup double cream

2 tbsp poppy seeds

3 eggs

3 tbsp lemon juice

1 tsp vanilla extract

Natural sweetener to taste

Directions

- Preheat the oven to 350.

- Combine the flour, flaxseed, erythritol, and seeds

- Melt the butter. Stir it into the flour with the cream and eggs. Create a smooth batter.

- Add the rest of the ingredients.

- Place 12 cupcake molds onto a baking tray and pour the mixture evenly into them. Silicone moulds are great for keeping the regular cost down.

- Bake for around 20 minutes, until brown. You can also do the skewer test previously mentioned.

- Allow to cool before serving.

PIZZA BREAKFAST FRITTATA

Ingredients

12 eggs

9oz spinach or baby spinach

1oz pepperoni

1 tsp garlic, minced

5oz mozzarella cheese

1/2 cup ricotta cheese

4 tbsp oil

1/4 tsp nutmeg

Seasoning to taste

Directions

- Preheat the oven to 375.

- Mix the eggs, spices, and oil together.

- Add in the cheese and spinach.

- Add to a skillet, sprinkle with some extra mozzarella cheese on top.

- Add the pepperoni or any other desire toppings.

- Place in the oven and bake for 30 minutes.

MOCK MCGRIDDLE LOAF

Ingredients

1 cup almond flour

1/4 cup flaxseed

1lb sausage

10 eggs

4oz cheese — cheddar or something similar

6 tbsp maple syrup

4 tbsp butter

1/2 tsp onion powder

1/2 tsp garlic powder

1/4 tsp sage

Seasoning to taste

Directions

- Pre-heat the oven to 350F degrees.

- Add the sausage to a pan on the stove. Break up and cook until brown

- Place all the dry ingredients into a bowl. Combine and add the wet ingredients, except for the 2 tbsp of maple syrup.

- Add the sausage.

- Place parchment paper into a casserole dish and add the mixture.

- Drizzle the remaining syrup.

- Bake for around 50 minutes, until completely cooked through.

- Remove and allow to cool.

Try serving with some syrup or ketchup. It's perfect for that Sunday morning treat.

CAULIFLOWER AND JALAPENO CHEESE

Ingredients for the puree

    1 cauliflower head

    2 tbsp double cream

    1 tbsp butter

    1/4 cup cheese grated

    1 tbsp jalapenos, chopped

    1/4 tsp garlic powder

    Seasoning to taste

Ingredients for the cheese

    6 oz cream cheese

    1/2 cup cheese, shredded

    1/4 cup of salsa

Ingredients for the topping

    3/4 cup Colby jack cheese, grated

    1/4 cup jalapenos, sliced

Directions

Puree

1. Preheat the oven at 375.

2. Break the cauliflower into medium sized pieces, then pop them in the microwave with the cream and butter for 10 minutes. Coat with the melted cream and butter and put in the microwave for another 6minutes.

3. Remove and place in a blender with the rest of the ingredients. Blend until pureed.

Cream cheese:

1. Place the cream cheese in a bowl and microwave for 30 seconds.

2. Add the cheese and salsa, mixing completely.

Casserole Assembly

1. Spread the puree across a casserole dish.

2. Spread the cream cheese over the top.

3. Layer with your toppings.

4. Bake for 20 minutes.

If you choose to add vegetables, do so with the cream cheese layer.

KETO FRIENDLY SUSHI

Ingredients

16 oz cauliflower

6 oz softened cream cheese

2 tbsp rice vinegar

5 nori sheets

1 tbsp soy sauce

1 mini cucumber

2 avocados

5 oz of seafood of your choice

Directions

1. Grate the cauliflower.

2. Slice the ends of your cucumber off and then slice it in half, discarding the middle (seeds) of both. Then, slice into strips and set to one side.

3. Add cauliflower into a very hot pan, seasoning with soy sauce as it cooks.

4. Add the cauliflower to a bowl and mix in the cream cheese and vinegar. Set in the fridge to cool.

5. Once the rice is cooled, slice your avocado into small strips and remove the shell.

6. Place a nori sheet onto your bamboo roller. Spread on the rice, leaving about 3/4in at the top.

7. Place your fillers, layering just the way you want.

8. Roll the sushi with your bamboo roller. This will take some practice to get right.

Serve with wasabi and pickled ginger. You'll feel like you're in a Japanese restaurant, enjoying a local dish.

CHOCOLATE AND COCONUT BARS

Ingredients

1 cup unsweetened coconut, desiccated

1 packet natural sweetener (stevia)

1 tsp vanilla extract

1/3 cup coconut cream

4 tbsp coconut oil/cocoa butter

2 tbsp cocoa powder, unsweetened

Directions

1. Mix the coconut, cream, extract, and stevia together, mixing with a spoon.

2. Line a cookie sheet with parchment paper and place the coconut mixture on it.

3. Shape mixture into a rectangle, about 1in thick.

4. Freeze for two hours or until solid.

5. As you wait for it to cool, melt your coconut oil/cocoa butter in a sauce pan.

6. Add the powder, natural sweetner, and extract the oil. Mix and heat for 2 minutes.

7. Allow to cool until it is room temperature.

8. Remove the coconut from the freezer and cut into bars.

9. Dip the bars into the cocoa mixture, coating all sides evenly.

10. Place onto the cookie sheet and put into the fridge to cool completely.

11. Allow to remain in the fridge to keep the solid consistency when it comes to eating them.

If you want them softer, allow them to reaching room temperature.

CHOCOLATE MUG CAKE

Ingredients

1 egg

2 tbsp butter

2 tbsp almond butter or protein powder

2 tbsp cocoa powder, unsweetened

1 1/2 tbsp Splenda

2 tsp coconut flour

1/4 tsp vanilla extract

1/2 tsp baking powder

Directions

- Grab a mug and put 2tbsp of butter into it.

- Microwave for about 25 seconds until the butter hot and melted. Next, add the sweetener.

- Add the cocoa powder, coconut and almond flours, extract, baking powder, and egg.

- Mix until completely combined. You'll need to make sure there are no lumps for this to turn out just right.

- Microwave for about 75 seconds.

489

You can also make whip cream in a mixing bowl while making the cake, just remember to allow the cake to cool before you add the whipped cream on top!

CHOCOLATE AND PEANUT BUTTER TARTS

Ingredients

Crust

   1/4 cup flaxseed ground until fine

   2 tbsp almond flour

   1 egg white

   1 tbsp sweetener

The middle layer

   4 tbsp peanut butter (or nut butter of your choice)

   2 tbsp butter

The top layer

   1 avocado

   4 tbsp cocoa powder, unsweetened

   1/4 cup sweetener

   1/2 tsp vanilla extract

   2 tbsp double cream

   1/2 cinnamon

Directions

1. Preheat the oven to 350F degrees.

2. Mix the ground flaxseeds and the rest of the crust ingredients until fully combined.

3. Press the mixture into a tart pan all the way up the sides.

4. Bake for 8 minutes until set.

5. Combine all the top layer ingredients in the blender. Smooth until creamy and set to one side.

6. Allow the crust to cool, while mixing your peanut butter and butter in the microwave.

7. Pour into the crust and refrigerate for 30 minutes until set.

8. Pour you top later over giving it a smooth texture and place in the fridge for an hour or so.

VEGAN POTATO NACHOS

Ingredients

3 cup potatoes, diced

1 jalapeno, thinly sliced

1 red pepper, finely chopped

1/2 cup pico de gallo

1 cup cooked black beans, (if canned, rinsed and drained)

salt and pepper to taste

1/4 tsp garlic powder

2 Tbsp nutritional yeast

1 tsp chili powder

1/4 cup dairy-free milk (unsweetened almond milk)

1/2 orange pepper, roughly chopped

1/3 cup cashews, soaked at least two hours

1 tsp cumin

1 Tbsp olive oil

Guacamole

Directions

Heat a cast iron pan to medium-high heat until it is very hot. Add oil and cook for 30 seconds then add potatoes and sprinkle with salt, pepper, and cumin. Cook, flipping occasionally, until crispy on all sides, about 15 minutes.

While the potatoes are cooking, make the cheese sauce. Place the cashews, orange pepper, milk, chili powder, nutritional yeast, garlic powder, and a pinch of salt/pepper in a blender. Puree until smooth, about 2-5 minutes depending on the blender being used. Blending for this long should make the cheese sauce hot, but if you want it hotter, you can heat up in the microwave or on the stove.

Layer the nachos: potatoes, cheese sauce, black beans, pico de gallo, chopped red pepper, sliced jalapenos, and guacamole.

MUSHROOM AND KALE ENCHILADAS WITH RED SAUCE

Ingredients

2 tbsp olive oil

1/4 tsp ground black pepper

3 oz dried California chili pods, stems and seeds removed

1/3 cup yellow onion, chopped

2 garlic cloves

2 cup vegetable broth

1 tbsp dried chili powder

1 tsp dried cumin

1 tsp flour

1 tsp sugar

1/2 tsp salt

Directions

Place a skillet on medium heat. When hot, add the dried pepper pods and cook on each side for 20-30 seconds. Make sure they do not burn.

Remove from the skillet and add to a saucepan filled with hot water. Make sure the water covers the peppers. Let stand for 15 minutes, then drain.

While the peppers are in the water, add the oil to a skillet over medium heat. When hot, add the onion and cook for 3-4 minutes, followed by the garlic for 30 seconds or until fragrant.

Add the flour to the skillet and whisk. Add the chili powder, cumin, salt, black pepper, sugar, and vegetable broth. Mix well. Reduce to low heat.

Add the drained peppers and the mixture from the skillet into a blender. Blend until smooth. Note: depending on your blender, you may need to strain the mixture through a mesh strainer and discard the solid pieces.

ENCHILADAS

Ingredients

1⁄4 cup yellow onion, diced

2 garlic cloves, minced

8 oz cremini mushrooms, cleaned and diced

3 cup (packed) chopped kale

1⁄4 tsp salt

1⁄4 tsp ground black pepper

6 (8-inch) flour tortillas

2 oz Cotija cheese to sprinkle over the top

Sour cream for garnish

2 tbsp olive oil

Fresh cilantro leaves for garnish

Directions

Preheat the oven to 325F degrees.

Add the olive oil to a skillet over medium heat. When hot, add the onion and cook for 3-4 minutes, or until the onion begins to soften. Add the garlic and cook for 30 seconds before adding the mushrooms. Add the salt and black pepper and cook, stirring, until the mushrooms begin to release their juices. Add the kale and cook, stirring occasionally, until it softens. Remove from the heat and set aside.

Add the red sauce to a shallow skillet or bowl and place near the mushroom and kale mixture. Add 2 tbsps of the red sauce to the bottom of a 9x9-inch baking pan and spread it across the bottom. Place the pan next to the filling mixture.

One by one, dip each tortilla into the red sauce to cover both sides. Let the excess sauce drip back into the skillet. You may need to use your fingers to help remove some of the excess sauce. Lay each sauce-coated tortilla on a flat surface like a clean cutting board. Add about 2 heaping tbsps of the mushroom and kale mixture across the bottom edge of each tortilla, and leave a bit of room on either side, and at the bottom.

Starting with the end with the filling, roll the tortilla tightly to the other end. Then, place the rolled tortillas in the baking dish, seam side down. Pour about half of the remaining enchilada sauce over the rolled tortillas.

Cover with foil and bake for 30 minutes. Remove from the oven. Serve warm on individual plates with extra sauce on the side.

Drizzle with sour cream and sprinkled with Cotija cheese and torn fresh cilantro.

SUPER EASY VEGGIE MAC AND CHEESE

Ingredients

1 lb macaroni or other small noodle

2 Tbsp butter

2 Tbsp flour

2 cup 2% milk

2 cup shredded sharp cheddar cheese

1 package Earthbound Farm frozen butternut squash, cooked and pureed until very smooth

Salt and pepper to taste

Optional: nutmeg

Directions

Cook pasta according to package directions.

Meanwhile, place butter in a large pot and heat over medium heat.

Once melted, sprinkle the flour on the butter and stir for 1-2 minutes.

Whisk in the milk, 1/2 cup at a time and cook until the

flour has disappeared into the milk and the   mixture has thickened, about 5 minutes, stirring constantly.

Stir in the pureed squash, then add the shredded cheese and continue to stir until mixture is smooth.

Season with salt, pepper, and nutmeg is desired.

When the pasta has finished cooking, drain and immediately mix into the cheese sauce.

Serve right away, with extra shredded cheese on top if desired.

WARM GREEN BEANS AND LETTUCE IN ANCHOVY BUTTER

Ingredients

4 Tbsp unsalted butter

Chopped pistachios, for garnish

1 scallion, thinly sliced

Pepper

Sea salt

2 Tbsp fresh lemon juice, plus lemon wedges for serving

4 heads Little Gem or baby romaine lettuce, quartered lengthwise

2 garlic cloves, minced

6 oil-packed anchovy fillets, drained and chopped

1 lb green beans, trimmed

Extra-virgin olive oil, for garnish

Directions

In a large skillet, melt 3 tbsps of the butter. Then, add

the green beans, anchovies and garlic and cook over moderate heat, stirring occasionally, until the beans are tender, about 5 minutes. Transfer the beans to a large plate.

Add the remaining 1 tbsp of butter and the lettuce to the skillet and cook, turning occasionally, until the lettuce is golden and crisp-tender, about 2 minutes. Add the green beans and lemon juice and season with salt and pepper; toss to coat. Transfer the beans and lettuce to a serving platter and top with the sliced scallion. Top with pistachios, drizzle with olive oil and serve warm with lemon wedges.

CONCLUSION

These recipes are a great way to get started with the vegetarian keto diet. They're not only fun and easy to make, but you'll barely notice the change. You'll be able to get your favourites like curries, sushi, pasta, and even sandwiches. With slight variations, you can cut out the carbs and focus on the fats that your body needs to create the ketones in the liver.

Go into this with full effort because you'll benefit from it in the end. Your mind will be in the zone, and you'll be able to enjoy a healthier lifestyle. Keep in mind that you're not saying "no" to anything, you're just finding ways to enjoy the things that you love without the things that are detrimental to your health.

Now that you've made the decision to follow the diet, it's time to choose the type.

When you want to add some carbs to a workout, you can follow the targeted ketogenic diet where you're allowed a few extra carbs, but only on the days and around the time of your workouts. After all, the focus is on still getting the exercise without struggling with energy. You wouldn't need to do this if you get enough fat into your diet and once your body gets into the ketone producing zone.

Now it's your turn – pick your diet and choose from the best vegeterian keto recipes for weight loss.